BISON
BOOKS

Benjamin Franklin
AND THE AMERICAN
REVOLUTION

JONATHAN R. DULL

UNIVERSITY OF NEBRASKA PRESS | LINCOLN & LONDON

Library of Congress Cataloging-in-Publication Data

Dull, Jonathan R., 1942–
Benjamin Franklin and the American Revolution / Jonathan R. Dull.
p. cm.
Includes bibliographical references and index.
ISBN 978-0-8032-3033-0 (pbk. : alk. paper)
1. Franklin, Benjamin, 1706–1790. 2. Diplomats—Great Britain—Biography.
3. United States—History—Revolution, 1775–1783. 4. United States—Foreign
relations—1775–1783. 5. Statesmen—United States—Biography. I. Title.
E302.6.F8D848 2010
973.3092—dc22
[B]
2010003779

Set in Swift EF by Bob Reitz.

Contents

Preface

I spent more than thirty years reading Benjamin Franklin's mail. From July 1977 until my retirement in June 2008, I helped to edit some 20 volumes of *The Papers of Benjamin Franklin*, an ongoing 47-volume edition of his writings and correspondence. While doing research on the letters he sent and received during the American Revolution, I often was struck by how one-sided is the traditional picture of Franklin, particularly during the Revolution. Most readers are quite familiar with his softer side—his affability, his flirting with the ladies of Paris during a nine-year diplomatic mission to France, his sense of humor, and his conciliatory nature, which so smoothed the working of the Franco-American alliance. All of this is true about him, but it is only half of the picture. It tends to make Franklin a bystander to the violence, danger, and suffering of the Revolution. Franklin actually was a leader of that revolution; indeed, with the exception of George Washington, he was its most irreplaceable leader. He could not have made this contribution to American independence without a lesser-known tougher side from which he drew his strength. The traditional picture of Franklin does not adequately portray his confidence and self-righteousness about himself and the American cause, his almost fanatical zeal, his hatred of George III and the king's American supporters (particularly Franklin's own son), his disdain for hardship and danger, and, finally, his vanity, pride, and ambition. This two-sided Franklin is not as lovable as the kindly and avuncular person of legend, but he is more complex, more interesting, and in many ways more impressive. This book will introduce you to him.

I could not have written this book without other Franklin scholars. The one I have known the longest is Robert Middlekauff, who taught me historiography when I was a graduate student at the University of California–Berkeley in 1968 and whose friendship I have treasured ever since. Upon arriving in New Haven in 1977 I became a colleague and friend of another great Franklinist, Claude-Anne Lopez. Eventually Claude became the second of the four chief editors of the Franklin Papers with whom I served. I learned a great deal not only from her but also from her predecessor, William B. Willcox, and her successors, Barbara Oberg and Ellen Cohn, as well as from current associate editor Kate Ohno and dozens of other associate editors, assistant editors, administrative assistants, and interns. I have also had the good fortune to cross paths with such superb Franklin scholars as Ed Morgan, the late Leo Lemay, Gordon Wood, Jim Hutson, Sheila Skemp, Stacy Schiff, David Waldstreicher, and Alan Houston. I wish particularly to thank Thomas Schaeper, who commented on the book in manuscript. Those from whom I have learned deserve credit for much of what is worthwhile about this book; its mistakes are my responsibility.

My greatest debt is to my family, particularly my incredibly supportive wife, Susan Kruger, my wonderful children, Veronica Lamka, Robert Dull, Max Kruger-Dull, and Anna Kruger-Dull, and my terrific sister, Caroline Hamburger, and nephews, Peter and John Hamburger. Through Susan I acquired an extended family who are very dear to me: Stan Kruger, the late Alice Kruger, Steven Kruger, Glenn Burger, Josh Kruger, Diane Bassett, David Kruger, and Jessica Kruger. I dare not forget those highly intelligent cats Big Spot and Little Spot, who can turn doorknobs and for all I know may be able to read this. To you all, love and thanks.

I dedicate this book in memory of two of the finest people I've ever known, my father, Earl Dull, and my mother-in-law, Alice Kruger.

BENJAMIN FRANKLIN AND THE AMERICAN REVOLUTION

Chapter One

From Rebelliousness to Prosperity

I

AS MANY SCHOLARS HAVE NOTED, Benjamin Franklin is perhaps the most challenging of the founding fathers to understand.[1] Even after thirty years of research I am not sure I really know him. He was very cautious about committing his feelings to writing and very good at keeping secrets. Relatively few of the letters he wrote during the first half of his life are extant, partly because British soldiers destroyed many of them. Franklin's parents and siblings provide us little evidence about his childhood and adolescence, so most of what we know about his early life is what he chose to tell us.[2]

One example of the difficulty this causes his biographers is how hard it is for us to account for his extreme distaste for direct confrontation and conflict. No doubt this was partly a matter of playing to his strengths. Much of his political success was based on his skill as a conciliator and consensus builder. His hatred of confrontation, however, sometimes led him to downplay genuine differences of opinion. He even claimed that he had no personal enemies.[3] Some of this undoubtedly was for the sake of public relations, such as his writing friends in Europe that the difficulties of America in the mid-1780s were not of importance.[4] His aversion to confrontation, however, seem to have been genuine. He reacted bitterly when his attempts to avoid conflict were thwarted; woe to those like Thomas Penn or King George III who rejected his peacemaking and thereby made themselves his enemies.[5] What, however, was the source of his feelings? They may have come from his being the fifteenth of his father's seventeen children (seven by his first wife, ten by his second). Members of large families have good reason to prize peace and quiet. We cannot know, however, if he had childhood memories too frightening or painful to confront or parts of himself he did not wish to acknowledge. What we do know is that he could be extremely defensive, perhaps even from himself.

II

In spite of his reserve we can state some things about him based on what he said or, better still, what he did. First, like many people, he resembled his father in numerous ways. He revealed his similarity to his father, Josiah Franklin, in his love for the things of the mind, in his dedication to public service, in his concern for justice and for the feelings of others, and in his essential decency. His father made candles and soap, whereas he helped make a revolution and a new country, but they both demonstrated their worth by serving others. We know less of Franklin's mother, Abiah, but she, too, lived a life of service to others, particularly her husband, children, and stepchildren.

In spirit, Franklin never totally left Boston, where he was born in 1706. He left there for good at age 17, returning only for visits. Thereafter he lived for long periods in Philadelphia, London, and Passy, a village near Paris. He also traveled frequently. As deputy postmaster general for the British North American colonies, he made inspection trips up and down their Atlantic coastline. While living in England he made a number of trips for pleasure across the British Isles and western Europe. Nevertheless he never fully shed his roots in Puritan Boston.

Like all good Puritans, he dedicated himself to a calling. His was the calling of printer-publisher-writer. There was printer's ink in his veins until he died at age 84. He never lost his love for printing presses, paper and ink, and the chance to occupy his pen. He even left behind a grandson to carry on his work, Benjamin Franklin Bache, the crusading editor of the *Philadelphia Aurora* during the 1790s.[6]

Also like a good Puritan, Franklin extolled the virtues of hard work and treated prosperity as a proof of one's merit. Although he enjoyed the company of women and children and treated them with uncommon respect for the time, his views of the family were characteristically paternalistic. He saw himself as the head of the family and expected to be treated as such. He did not attend his son William's wedding when his son chose his own wife; worse still, when William, who had been appointed governor of New Jersey in 1762, elected to remain loyal to the king rather than join his father as a revolutionary, Benjamin treated it as a personal betrayal. On the other hand, his daughter Sally, a woman of extraordinary warmth, kindness, and generosity, apparently never stopped loving him; he spent the last five years of his life with her, his son-in-law, and his grandchildren in the house he had built for his wife. Sally, who knew him so well, is his best character reference.

He loved the sensual pleasures of the dinner table and the marital bed, but this was not unusual even for Puritan Boston. What made him rather unusual for a Bostonian were his radical religious beliefs, such as his belief in the basic equality of different religions. These beliefs, however, were not uncommon for members of the American upper class.[7] He did not much concern himself with the state of his soul, but he did preach the existence of an afterlife and the importance of leading a life of benevolence toward others.

Franklin had a very successful career. His first job was as an apprentice in his brother's printing shop, a job that made him so unhappy that he fled Boston. He lived by his wits and skills until he acquired his own printing shop and purchased a newspaper to print. Aided greatly by his industrious, talented, and loyal wife he became prosperous enough to retire from business just before his 42nd birthday. He dedicated himself thereafter to science, politics, and writing, passing much of the second half of his life abroad.

On some matters, such as slavery, his attitudes evolved over his lifetime.[8] On many others he continued in the same beliefs in spite of the many changes in his life.[9] He was a lifelong supporter of population growth as the key to America's prosperity. So, too, was he an advocate of free trade and, a rather different proposition, of a plentiful supply of paper money to encourage economic growth. He never liked bicameral legislatures, believing that they led to political paralysis; he was particularly opposed to legislative upper houses reserved for the wealthy.[10] He was a lifelong supporter of prison reform, and he devoted enormous effort to helping American prisoners of war being held in England or Ireland.

His views were a mixture of what today we would call liberalism and conservatism, which helps account for his political success at the time and his almost universal popularity today. This in part was because he sometimes considered himself an outsider and sometimes an insider, as good a way as any to differentiate liberals from conservatives. He had a strong dislike of mobs, whether they were formed of London workers, embittered frontiersmen like the Paxton Boys of 1762, or angry farmers like the 1786 Massachusetts followers of Daniel Shays.[11] He had little sympathy for the unemployed, not understanding that there might be reasons beyond their control to account for their joblessness. On the other hand, Franklin never forgot that he was the son of a tradesman. He despised the idle rich as much as he scorned the idle poor, although he enjoyed the company and hospitality of those he believed had earned their fortune; he even argued that unneeded private property rightly was the property of the public.[12] Like Thomas Jefferson he praised the common man and maintained lifelong friendships with people who worked with their hands as he once had done and hence were not gentlemen (although such friendships gradually became less common). Unlike Jefferson, however, Franklin always lived in or near cities. His support for those who worked the land was mostly theoretical and was not unrelated to his involvement in land speculation. One of his strongest prejudices was against uncouth and uneducated farmers and frontiersmen, particularly those of German origin. In a 1782 note he composed for himself, he described frontiersmen as the most disorderly of people and criticized them for committing offenses against their neighbors and occasioning disputes between the states.[13] On the other hand, he was remarkably free of religious prejudice; according to John Adams, Catholics, Anglicans, Presbyterians, and Quakers all considered him one or virtually one of their own.[14]

For Franklin, the American Revolution was the culmination of a long process of finding where he truly belonged. He discovered easily enough that he was not just a Pennsylvanian but a British American. It took many years for him finally to accept that he would have to choose between being British or American. To his great sadness he learned that to the wealthy and powerful of Great Britain he was an outsider. His own subsequent rejection of Britain was not merely personal; Franklin did not become a revolutionary out of spite. The British government rejected the social class from which he had come, the Philadelphia and Pennsylvania political institutions he had served, and the ideals of self-government and reasoned compromise to which he had devoted his life. Franklin lived in England from 1724 to 1726, 1757 to 1762, and late 1764 to 1775. He so loved the country and its people that he considered spending his retirement there, but it is highly unlikely the British government could ever have won or purchased his support in its attempts to weaken American self-government.

Franklin spent his last year in London attempting to prevent revolution, but once he returned to America he became as zealous a revolutionary as anyone. The Loyalists (those Americans who remained loyal to the king) considered him the arch-conspirator.[15] To America's good fortune, Franklin's experiences turned him into an exceptionally useful revolutionary. Both his virtues and his vices proved serviceable: his political acumen, his genius for public relations, his secretiveness, his deviousness, his unshakable confidence in himself and in the American cause, his willingness to sacrifice for the cause, and, when necessary, his ruthlessness. Before examining further his contribution to the Revolution, let us examine how his experiences helped prepare him to be a revolutionary.

III

Franklin's father inadvertently pushed him toward becoming a rebel, the first stage of becoming a revolutionary. In 1714–15 Benjamin attended the South Grammar School (now Boston Latin). The 8-year-old was a bright student and seemingly was destined for Harvard College and a place among the elite of Massachusetts. Josiah Franklin prevented it. Although a respected member of the community and his church, he was only a tradesman with a large family to support.

After his son completed his first year of school, Josiah Franklin decided he could not afford the academic education that was a prerequisite for entering Harvard. Instead he gave him a year of training in mathematics and other practical skills before putting him to work in his own business, helping to turn animal fat into soap and candles. He was not unkind, however. When he saw how much Benjamin hated the unpleasant work, he allowed the young man to choose his own apprenticeship in which he would be taught a trade in exchange for years of service to a master.

In 1718 Benjamin made his choice, one that eventually would lead him to prosperity, an early retirement, and then fame. He was apprenticed to his 21-year-old brother James, who had just returned from England with a printing press. The best route to success for a printer was to begin a newspaper, and in 1721 James Franklin launched the *New-England Courant*. James was not exactly a crusading journalist, but his paper was lively and controversial. James became in some ways a role model for his younger brother, but their relationship had serious problems, as relationships between brothers often do. In the case of the Franklins a good part of the difficulty was that James had the legal power to enforce his apprentice's obedience, but Benjamin was equally ambitious, more intelligent, and a far better writer than was his older brother. In April 1722 he slipped a newspaper essay signed by an obviously fictitious Silence Dogood under the door of his brother's newspaper office, the first of fourteen essays published over the course of the year. The essays were a success, and James did not guess that their author was his 16-year-old brother. Not surprisingly, the fourth of the essays was a satire on the education of Harvard students.[16]

Franklin's mocking of elitist Harvard students was not just sour grapes. He took a serious interest in the content and purpose of higher education. In 1749, now living in Philadelphia, he drafted a prospectus for an academy or college (a college that eventually became the University of Pennsylvania). His *Proposals Relating to the Education of Youth in Pennsylvania* were revolutionary. They called for students to be taught useful subjects like arithmetic, accounting, geometry, history, and geography, a curriculum different from the traditional one centered around the study of Greek and Roman authors.[17]

Benjamin eventually confessed to writing the Dogood essays. Having such a talented, devious, and cocky younger brother and apprentice was not easy for James, either. He beat Benjamin, and their relationship deteriorated. In 1723 Benjamin ran away from his brother and thereby violated the terms of his apprenticeship contract, a serious breach of the law. (Apprentices were considered servants by the law; if they were caught running away, their term of servitude was extended.)[18] He first fled to New York, but failing to find work he proceeded to Philadelphia. Although he arrived virtually penniless, he had training in a skilled craft, his wit, and his self-confidence. It did not take long for him to find a job and then an influential patron, Sir William Keith, the lieutenant governor of Pennsylvania. Keith promised to lend him the money to set up his own printing shop. Confidently, Franklin sailed to England to purchase printing supplies. He arrived only to find that Keith had not provided the money he had promised. Again Franklin, forced to live by his wits, found work as a printer. After nearly two years in London he returned to Philadelphia in 1726.[19]

The experience was a lesson about not putting too much trust in those in power. Its immediate influence can be overestimated, however. Franklin retained his trust in the kings of England, if not their government officials, for almost another half-century. He continued to depend on the patronage of the powerful and wealthy and eventually extended his own patronage in turn to his relatives and apprentices, setting them up in their own printing shops in exchange for a share of their profits. After being appointed deputy postmaster general, he again used his patronage on behalf of relatives and clients.

To be dependent on others does not seem to have been very pleasant for him, however. He constructed for an English and American audience (and perhaps for himself) an idealized America where such dependence was unnecessary. In 1751 he wrote an essay entitled "Observations Concerning the Increase of Mankind" in response to an act of Parliament restricting expansion of the American iron industry. Franklin portrayed the British colonies in North America as a land of small farmers in which abundant cheap land permitted universal financial independence, if not prosperity.[20] Like Thomas Jefferson's later vision of America, this was an eloquent statement of what has become our core belief about ourselves, "the American dream." Franklin's essay was splendid propaganda, but it ignored not only the social turbulence of American seaports like Philadelphia and the ever-present possibility of slave revolts but also pockets of social conflict that would spread during the next twenty-five years throughout the colonies, from the Green Mountains of what today is Vermont to the manors of the Hudson River valley to the backcountry of North and South Carolina.[21] Nothing could shake Franklin's vision, however. In 1784 he wrote a similar essay for prospective American immigrants, "Information to Those Who Would Remove to America."[22]

Seeing America not just as a prospective utopia but as one already in existence made Franklin sensitive to those in Britain who would despoil it. An example of Franklin's protectiveness about America is a short newspaper article he wrote in 1751, "Rattle-Snakes for Felons." Outraged at a proposal to deport convicted English criminals to the American colonies, Franklin proposed returning the favor by sending rattlesnakes in exchange, particularly to St. James's Park in London and to the gardens of prime ministers, members of the Board of Trade, and members of Parliament.[23]

This article did not raise what would become a critical issue for Franklin, the right of Parliament to legislate for the American colonies. It did, however, challenge the notion that the colonies were subordinate to Great Britain itself. In contrast, Franklin's "Observations" were both imperial and mercantilist. The

British Crown and its instruments, such as the British navy, held the empire together, but the American colonies were a vital and growing part of that empire. In particular, their trade with the home island was vital to its prosperity and hence to the power of the Crown; Franklin especially stressed the American contribution to British naval power.

IV

By the time Franklin wrote his 1751 essay and article, he was no longer a struggling tradesman but a wealthy, recently retired printer and newspaper editor. His success began with two wise decisions early in his career. The first was in 1729, when he took over a failing newspaper, the *Pennsylvania Gazette*, which he turned into the most influential journal in the British colonies. The second was in 1730, when he entered a common-law marriage with Deborah Read, the daughter of his former landlord. She proved not only an affectionate and loyal wife but a key part of Franklin's financial success. Extremely hardworking, she ran the hugely successful stationery and bookstore on the ground floor of their house, while he ran the newspaper and print shop upstairs.[24]

Owning a print shop and newspaper permitted Benjamin to publicize a number of civic improvement projects he helped to establish, as well as aiding him to enter into Pennsylvania politics. He had an extraordinary gift as an organizer, being able to cajole associates, disarm potential opposition, and hide his powerful ambition and vanity behind compliments and good fellowship. The organizations he helped to found are a testament to his civic spirit and concern for the common good. He founded or helped to found a fraternal organization to discuss practical and ethical questions (the Junto), a volunteer fire company, a lending library, a fire insurance company, a college, a scientific society, and a hospital.[25] This hardly seems the work of a revolutionary, but in a number of ways his civic projects helped prepare him for his role in the American Revolution. First, they taught him not to rely on established governments like that of Britain or Pennsylvania. Most of his various voluntary associations were, at least at first, outside of government interference, particularly the interference of the descendants of William Penn. As proprietors of Pennsylvania acting as deputies of the British Crown, the Penns had the right to appoint a governor with veto power over the acts of the Pennsylvania Assembly. Eventually Franklin turned to the governor, assembly, or city of Philadelphia for assistance with such major projects as the hospital and college, but with results that were not totally satisfactory. In contrast, his purely voluntary associations taught him that the common people could be entrusted with organizing common affairs. They also reinforced the egalitarian side of his personality. Finally, they helped give him confidence and vital experience in organizing institutions from scratch, a central task of the American Continental Congress after the Battles of Lexington and Concord. One of his civic institutions even helped prepare for another key part of the Continental Congress's task, that of supervising the revolution's military operations. In 1747–48, the last years of King George's War (known in Europe as the War of the Austrian Succession), the port of Philadelphia was threatened by French and Spanish privateers (privately owned but state-sanctioned warships used mostly to capture merchant ships). When the Pennsylvania Assembly, dominated by Quaker pacifists, failed to respond to the threat, Franklin helped organize a voluntary militia called the Association to defend the city.[26] During the next war, the so-called French and Indian War of 1754–60 (part of the Seven Years' War, which lasted until 1763), he helped obtain wagons for General Braddock's 1755 expedition against Fort Duquesne. The following year he was in command of building several forts in Northampton County, Pennsylvania.[27] Thus it is not surprising that in October 1775 Congress sent him as part of a committee that met with General Washington in Cambridge, Massachusetts, to devise regulations for the Continental army.[28]

Franklin's success as a revolutionary was grounded, of course, not only in his experiences in civic enterprises but also in his political experience. It was a natural evolution to move from civic activity to political activity, but it was Franklin's work as a printer that gave him an entry into politics. He was appointed printer to the Pennsylvania Assembly in 1730. An enthusiastic advocate of paper currency, he obtained his first contract to print currency (for New Jersey) in 1736. Later that same year he was selected as clerk to the Pennsylvania Assembly. He served for fifteen years, performing a number of important administrative functions, including printing the votes and acts of the assembly. He also publicized its activities in his newspaper.[29] His services to the assembly brought him friends, his conciliatory nature made him acceptable to all parties, and his retirement from the printing business gave him the leisure to devote himself to politics. It is not surprising that in 1751 he was elected to the assembly and resigned as its clerk. What is surprising is that politics soon would take him away from Philadelphia and back to England.

Two Missions to England

I

FRANKLIN HAD ALMOST twenty-five years of political experience when the American Revolution began. Most important were his missions to England on behalf of the Pennsylvania Assembly from 1757 to 1762 and from the end of 1764 to 1775. These missions were almost complete failures, partly because of Franklin's inexperience and poor judgment. In several ways, however, they were a vital prelude to his services to the American Revolution. First, in spite of Franklin's failures, his missions added to his reputation outside Philadelphia, transforming him from a local politician into a figure of great importance to all of the American colonies. Second, the experience he gained and the lessons he learned from his failure were of enormous help to him, particularly during his nine-year mission to France (from late 1776 until the middle of 1785) on behalf of Congress. Third, his missions reinforced his loyalty to America and cured him of the illusion that he could preserve his ideals while still being accepted by the wealthy and powerful of England. Fourth, the missions toughened him and helped make him a revolutionary. The zealous and angry Franklin of 1775 with his openness to change and democracy was partly the product of failure and rejection, which motivated him to embrace the dangers and challenges of making a revolution.

II

Franklin began his career in the Pennsylvania Assembly as someone outside of its two parties (or, more accurately, factions) that in the middle of the eighteenth century contended for political power. He initially was acceptable to both groups because of his industriousness, skill at building compromise, and writing ability. The majority party in the assembly was controlled by the Quakers. Although they were no longer the dominant religion in Pennsylvania, they were trusted politically by members of Pennsylvania's numerous other religions, such as the Anglicans, Presbyterians, and various German sects. The members of the rival group were supporters of the proprietors. The proprietors were descendants of William Penn, the Quaker who in 1681 had received the proprietorship of Pennsylvania from King Charles II of England; in exchange for founding the new colony he received the disposition of its land and virtual control over its government. Penn, however, promised those who purchased land from him a considerable measure of self-government. When he died, he left a disputed inheritance. This created a temporary power vacuum that the assembly, Pennsylvania's instrument of self-government, was able to fill. By 1751, when Franklin was elected to the assembly, the proprietorship was firmly in the control of Thomas Penn, a younger son of William Penn living in England. He sought to regain some of the power the Penn family had lost, but his party in the assembly was small, disunited, and disdainful of campaigning for votes.

During his first few years as assemblyman, Franklin stayed on good terms with both parties, while he made himself useful by writing committee reports. In 1753 Penn used his influence (or so he claimed) to support the appointment of Franklin as deputy postmaster general of the American colonies. Franklin, however, already had become disillusioned with Penn. Although Penn remained in England, he used the governors whom he appointed to obstruct the assembly on a number of issues dear to Franklin's heart, such as the issuance of paper money. To Penn, politics was subordinate to his private economic interest. Pennsylvania was the chief source of his income. The task of the governors he appointed was to protect and increase that income. For Franklin, the task of the governor, no less than the assembly, was to serve the public good. He felt it was wrong for the proprietor to issue binding instructions to the governor in his own interest rather than that of the people of Pennsylvania. This fundamental disagreement gradually turned Franklin and Penn into enemies.[1]

The most immediate issue was Penn's obstructionism when it came to the defense of Pennsylvania. The unsettled western part of Pennsylvania was claimed by both Virginia and New France (most of whose inhabitants lived between Montreal and Quebec) as well as by Pennsylvania. The Ohio Company, a group of land speculators that included the lieutenant governor of Virginia, attempted to forestall the governor general of New

France by building a fort at the forks of the Ohio, the site of present-day Pittsburgh. The French Canadians drove off the Virginians and began their own fort. Thereupon a body of volunteer troops from Virginia, commanded by the young George Washington, ambushed one of their patrols. The French Canadians soon returned in force and drove away the Virginians.[2] As this was occurring in the summer of 1754, Franklin and other colonial representatives were meeting at Albany with representatives of the Iroquois, a powerful confederation of six Indian nations. Franklin proposed that for the purposes of common defense, the governments of the British colonies should surrender some of their powers to a president general appointed by the British Crown and a grand council appointed by the various colonial assemblies. His plan was not seriously considered in either Britain or America. Fearful that the Quakers would not provide for the defense of Pennsylvania, he was willing temporarily to weaken local self-government for the sake of security and intercolonial unity, but few Americans agreed.[3]

Pennsylvania was in particular danger. The French Canadians were allied with numerous Indian nations, including the Delaware, who a few years earlier had been defrauded by Thomas Penn.[4] The British government moved quickly to gain control of the area. It sent two regiments under Gen. Edward Braddock to Virginia with orders to seize Fort Duquesne, the new French fort at the forks of the Ohio; they arrived early in 1755. Braddock expected the American colonists to provide wagons to haul supplies while he built a road from Virginia into western Pennsylvania. The Pennsylvania

Assembly, however, was unable to issue paper money to pay for wagons; the governor appointed by Penn would not approve a bill to issue it unless Penn had a share in deciding how the money raised would be appropriated. Similarly, the assembly did not increase taxes because Penn resisted its attempt to tax his lands. Franklin blamed Penn for the impasse and organized the requisition of wagons on the promise of his being repaid later.[5] The Quakers cooperated with Franklin; hard-line Quaker pacifists eventually resigned their seats in the assembly so that moderates could appropriate money for defense. Penn in turn offered a voluntary contribution for defense in order to exempt his lands from taxation. The French Canadians, however, were not as cooperative. On July 9, 1755, they and their Indian allies attacked Braddock's troops as they approached Fort Duquesne. Braddock was killed, and most of his troops were killed or wounded. The remnants of his force fled to Philadelphia, leaving the frontier open to Indian attack. A month earlier, a British squadron had fired on French ships bringing troops to Canada.[6] Although war was not formally declared until early the following year, Pennsylvania was now engaged in the most terrible conflict in its history. Franklin would be involved not only in this military conflict against France but also in the political conflict against Thomas Penn.

III

Franklin's assistance to General Braddock greatly increased his prestige and his importance in the Pennsylvania Assembly. Once the hard-line Quakers were replaced by members willing to accept war measures, Franklin became the informal leader of the assembly. He made defense of the colony his chief priority. Not only did he spend much of the winter of 1755–56 supervising the construction of forts, but he also persuaded the assembly to pass a militia act that included giving troops a role in electing their officers. Franklin was elected colonel of the Pennsylvania Regiment, the same rank held by George Washington in Virginia.

Ironically, Franklin's assistance to Braddock further poisoned his own relations with Penn. Jealous of the praise given to Franklin, Penn snubbed him by refusing to communicate with him, and Franklin responded in kind. More than personal feelings were involved, however. Penn still refused to approve taxes levied by the assembly, insisting that his property be exempted. The Quakers retaliated by blaming the troubles on the frontier on Penn's duplicity toward the Delaware nation. The military situation continued to be very serious, as even powerful Fort Granville was captured in August 1756.[7]

The assembly became convinced that only in England could the stalemate be resolved, and it selected Franklin to break the deadlock. In June 1757 he sailed for England.

Franklin had some grounds for believing in his own importance. Once he retired from business, he occupied himself not only with politics but also with conducting scientific experiments. His discoveries, particularly about electricity, and his inventions, such as the lightning rod, quickly made him the most famous scientist in America.[8] Moreover, his military activities had made him many friends, including Braddock's immediate successor as military commander in America, Governor William Shirley of Massachusetts. Nevertheless Franklin made several miscalculations. He underestimated Thomas Penn, who was shrewder and better connected with the English political and social establishment than Franklin realized. Conversely, he overestimated his own reputation among the English establishment, which with rare exceptions had as little an interest in science as it had in colonial politics. He also overestimated the degree of support he had among Quakers in England and America; he was regarded as an ally by many Quakers, but he had enemies as well, particularly among those who considered supporting war as the ultimate betrayal of their principles. Perhaps most important, Franklin placed too much trust in the British government and institutions. Britain was more a bastion of privilege than of self-government, as Franklin came to realize. Only a small minority of Englishmen could vote for members of the House of Commons, and access to real power was restricted to the wealthy and well-born. Furthermore, few Britons had any interest in the well-being of colonial subjects beyond seeing that they continued to enrich Britain by their trade. In fact, the tide was running against the colonists even before the outbreak of the recent war. The Board of Trade and its leader, George Montagu Dunk, Earl of Halifax, were opposed to the laxness of colonial administration and the degree of autonomy enjoyed by the North American colonies. The war caused the postponement of their plans to impose more central control over colonial legislatures, however. During the hostilities the Americans annually raised a large number of troops; by the climactic years of the war against the French, there were almost as many provincial troops serving in North America as there were British regulars. Secretary of State William Pitt, who served with one brief interruption from late 1756 to late 1761, had the good sense to reimburse colonial legislatures for some of their expenditures and to let them raise their own troops. During Pitt's years in office, the British took Canada and made a start on capturing the French West Indies.[9]

Americans and Britons shared common war aims, particularly the elimination of the French threat. This obscured real differences in their views on the proper nature of their relationship. Even Pitt's support for colonial legislatures was based solely on pragmatism; Franklin's assumption that Pitt would provide a sympathetic ear was naïve. Once the war ended, the British government would immediately abandon its policy of "salutary neglect" of its North American colonies, a policy that informally had given them a large measure of self-government.

Franklin thus sailed for England in 1757 much as he had in 1725, full of illusions about his ability to charm the powerful into assisting him. They would disappoint him just as Lieutenant Governor Keith had done. Franklin devoted much time and effort to negotiating with Thomas Penn. During their negotiations Penn mockingly told him that William Penn's charter allowing Pennsylvania immigrants political power was invalid. Franklin subsequently wrote to friends in Pennsylvania about his hatred and contempt for the younger Penn, an indiscretion that soon reached the current proprietor. Franklin's inability to control his emotions doomed any hope of compromise with Penn.[10]

Franklin had little more luck with the British government, particularly the Privy Council, which in 1760 rejected his proposal to turn Pennsylvania over to the Crown. This would have led to the replacement of the proprietor by a royal governor.[11] Franklin, however, did eventually score a great personal success, which probably accounts for his continued illusions about the benevolence of the British government and the degree of his own influence. As his wife, Deborah, was unwilling to leave Philadelphia, he was accompanied in England by his beloved son William, born out of wedlock in 1728 or 1729. In 1762 Franklin's friend Sir John Pringle, the physician of Prime Minister John Stuart, Earl of Bute, approached Bute on William Franklin's behalf. Bute obliged him by naming the young Franklin governor of the Crown colony of New Jersey. This was regarded as a great compliment to Benjamin Franklin, who had been tarrying in England, partly on his son's behalf. Franklin's feelings may have been more ambivalent; although he was a loving father, he was also very controlling and may not have completely welcomed his son's newfound independence. When William chose his own bride, the daughter of a West Indies planter, rather than one picked out for him by his father, Franklin abruptly left England for America in August 1762, thereby missing the wedding.[12] Disappointed at the failure of his mission and sad to leave the many friends he had made in England, he said that he expected to return soon. Barely two years later he came back. This second mission finally would cure him of his illusions.

IV

Franklin returned to Philadelphia just as the Franco-Spanish peace negotiations with Britain were concluding in Paris. In theory, the peace agreement that was reached in 1762 and formalized the following year should have brought peace and security to the Pennsylvania frontier. Franklin had reason to be pleased. He had written a pamphlet in 1760 urging Britain to retain Canada and return to France the valuable island of Guadeloupe, which Britain had recently captured. (Too much credit should not be given to Franklin and other pamphleteers for the decision to keep Canada, as it was based less on public opinion than on diplomatic necessity; France was willing to accept the loss of Canada, but was not willing to make peace without the return of its colonies in the West Indies.)[13] Except for what the French had successfully claimed was the "island" of New Orleans, all of America east of the Mississippi now was British. In fact, the apparently total British victory was hollow. As Franklin eventually would learn, the war permanently disrupted relations between Britain and its colonies. More immediately, the terms of peace brought new bloodshed to the frontier, particularly in Pennsylvania. Various Indian nations had made peace with Britain in 1758–59 on the understanding that the British would leave their hunting grounds as soon as Canada surrendered. Instead, the British not only refused to leave when Canada surrendered in 1760 but also built a huge new fort, Fort Pitt, at the site of Fort Duquesne and took possession of French Canadian trading posts like Detroit. The brutal British army commandant in North America, Gen. Jeffrey Amherst, treated Native Americans with contempt and refused to supply the trade goods on which they were dependent. Finally, news arrived that France had surrendered all its claims on the continent of North America. The French territory west of the Mississippi was being transferred to Spain in order to procure Spanish agreement to the peace. In the summer of 1763, a huge confederation of Indian nations rose in rebellion, capturing virtually all the British posts west of the line of white settlement except for Fort Pitt and Detroit.[14]

The subsequent war, named after Pontiac, one of its leaders, was particularly disruptive to Pennsylvania. Settlers along the frontier were incensed at the Quaker-dominated Pennsylvania Assembly, which was involved in a new dispute with Penn and hence had difficulty raising money for their defense. They also resented that the older counties along the Delaware River elected proportionally far more representatives to the assembly than did the newer counties to the west. Unsuccessful in defending themselves from Indian raiders, they took revenge by murdering nearby unarmed Native Americans who had converted to Christianity and were under government protection.

These frontiersmen, called the Paxton Boys, thereafter marched on Philadelphia to obtain redress of their grievances. The governor of Pennsylvania turned for help to Franklin, who organized a militia that saved the city and forced the Paxton Boys to disband. An outraged Franklin wrote "A Narrative of the Late Massacres, in Lancaster County, of A Number of Indians, Friends of this Province, by Persons Unknown."[15] This work displays an increasing humanitarianism and hatred of violence; during the same period, Franklin took halting steps toward recognizing the common humanity of whites and blacks.[16] On the other hand, Franklin's narrative also displays elitism and a failure to recognize the frontiersmen's grievances.

Franklin continued to idealize Britain, a common feeling in the afterglow of the British victorious war against the French, during which the British army and navy had come to the assistance of the American colonies.[17] Unwisely, he resurrected his plan to replace proprietary government with direct government by the British Crown. By 1764 many Americans had come to distrust the British government, fearing among other things the establishment of Anglicanism as a state religion in America as it was in England. Moreover, many Presbyterians were angry that the Quakers had blamed them for the Paxton Boys troubles because most of the Paxton Boys were Presbyterians. Members of the Proprietary Party saw their chance to harm the Quakers and their ally Franklin. For the assembly election of 1764, they made particular efforts to recruit candidates of German origin and gleefully recounted

Franklin's warning in his 1751 "Observations Concerning the Increase of Mankind" that the immigration into Pennsylvania of "Palatine Boors" could lead to the establishment of the German language and manners, the Palatine Boors in question being emigrants from the Palatinate, an area along the Rhine River.[18] Although the Quakers maintained a majority, albeit a reduced one, in the assembly, Franklin, running as a candidate in both the city and county of Philadelphia, was defeated.[19]

Undaunted, the assembly again voted to send Franklin to England. He sailed from Philadelphia on November 7, 1764, his wife again refusing to accompany him. This trip would nearly destroy his political career.

V

The Pennsylvania Assembly had learned at least one lesson from the failure of Franklin's first mission to England. During 1765, direct negotiations with Thomas Penn were left to English Quakers, while Franklin worked to establish good relations with Prime Minister George Grenville in case of their failure.[20] Grenville, however, had more pressing concerns than those of Pennsylvania. The war with France had led to a terrifying increase in the British national debt, while the war with Pontiac, recently concluded with a compromise peace settlement, had bolstered the British decision to keep a substantial number of troops in North America.[21] Desperate for revenue, Grenville insisted that the American colonies pay for maintaining the troops. Franklin suggested to him that he authorize the issuing of currency, thereby raising revenue for Britain while assisting the growth of the colonial economy. Instead, Grenville pushed through Parliament the Stamp Act, which taxed stamps used in various legal transactions and other items such as playing cards. Franklin, anxious to curry favor with Grenville, not only suggested to Americans that they cooperate but recommended agents to supervise collection of the taxes. Grenville honored the suggestions, using his patronage in accordance with Franklin's requests.[22]

In his obsession with Thomas Penn, Franklin had lost touch with American public opinion. The British government decided that levying direct taxes and bypassing colonial legislatures would be the simplest and most efficient way of collecting revenue. Many Americans, however, considered this a deliberate attempt to emasculate colonial legislatures, whose power was grounded in their ability (with the approval of the Crown) to collect and disburse tax revenues. In its contempt for American public opinion, the British government failed to woo the support of colonial leaders.[23] Americans protested in unprecedented numbers, forcing stamp distributors, including Pennsylvania nominee John Hughes, to resign. A mob even threatened Franklin's house, which was spared only because of the resistance of Deborah Franklin and Franklin's Philadelphia friends. What defeated the Stamp Act, however, was a boycott of British goods organized by American merchants. Grenville resigned in mid-1765, and his successor, Charles Watson-Wentworth, Marquess of Rockingham, successfully legislated repeal of the act.

In the process, Rockingham used Franklin to answer stage-managed questions about the act in the House of Commons.[24]

Franklin's change of heart seems to have been genuine, but it also had its pragmatic side. With Grenville out of office, he had no reason to support the act. By supporting its repeal he could begin to restore his reputation with his American constituents and build a good relationship with Rockingham and his supporters. Still believing in George III's good intentions, he also took care not to alienate the British Crown, even though there was no longer any hope of obtaining royal government for Pennsylvania. Moreover, Franklin had not lost interest in American expansion. Although he was a long-standing advocate of the Quaker policy of dealing fairly with Indians, he also favored establishing new colonies by purchasing Indian land. Soon he became involved in a massive western land scheme to accomplish this and enrich himself in the process; the proposed colony near the Ohio River in which he invested required the approval of the British government. Franklin, who had considerable knowledge of Indian affairs, turned a blind eye to the fact that purchasing land from them invariably involved fraud.

Franklin's role in the repeal of the Stamp Act marked a change in his political life. Thereafter he increasingly acted as a watchdog for American interests and a propagandist for the cause of colonial self-government under the authority of the king. During the repeal campaign he worked closely with the agents of other colonial legislatures. These agents, some of whom were English, sometimes acted almost like diplomats, negotiating on behalf of their colonies with the British government on such issues as reimbursement for the expenses incurred during the Seven Years' War. For the most part, however, they acted as lobbyists, seeking the support of members of Parliament and members of the government. Sadly, their victory in the campaign to repeal the Stamp Act was their last. All too soon there was a new administration and new taxes, the Townshend Acts of 1767.[25]

The surest path to reinforcing belief in one's religion or cause is to engage in its practice. Franklin was now regarded by the British government as an American, and he acted accordingly. He was so energetic in the American cause, particularly in writing newspaper articles, that various colonial assemblies appointed him as their agent: Georgia in 1768, New Jersey in 1769, Massachusetts in 1770. Consequently, the affairs of Pennsylvania, which lagged behind many other colonies in resistance to the British government, receded in importance to him. Franklin's relationship with the British government continued to deteriorate. First the proprietor, then Parliament, now even the cabinet—all seemed to him to sacrifice American rights to their own interests. The Earl of Hillsborough, British secretary of state for the colonies from 1768 to 1772, refused to accept Franklin's credentials from Massachusetts and generally treated him with contempt. Franklin was outraged at Hillsborough's conceit, but he was not yet ready to abandon his faith in George III. In a 1770 letter to his friend Samuel Cooper, he claimed that only the king had authority over the American colonies. He praised George's "good disposition" toward the American colonies, but did not yet admit that the king, financially dependent on Parliament, could not act in America's defense (and, in fact, had no disposition to do so).[26]

Franklin tended to see the growing split between Britons and British Americans not as the result of incompatible economic and political interests but as the result of deliberate attempts by ill-intentioned men to sow disunion. He saw Lt. Gov. Thomas Hutchinson of Massachusetts as the chief conspirator. When someone, still unknown, gave him copies of inflammatory letters written by Hutchinson and his ally, Massachusetts secretary Andrew Oliver, Franklin sent them to members of the Massachusetts legislature. Against Franklin's instructions, the letters were leaked to the press and printed. Rather than have someone else be blamed, Franklin courageously admitted his role. In January 1774 he was humiliated before the Privy Council in a meeting room called the Cockpit; he chose to remain silent while being called a thief. He then was dismissed as deputy postmaster general, and he pretended to resign as a member of the company seeking a western land grant. (The application eventually failed anyway.)[27] Although the humiliation in the Cockpit embittered Franklin, it was merely the culmination of a process of disillusionment about the British government that had begun far earlier. Franklin had long since decided where his loyalties lay. He still cared enough about Britain, though, to try to prevent his having to choose

sides. He spent much of his last year in Britain attempting to resolve a final crisis. This crisis was caused by
the Boston Tea Party, news of which reached England
shortly before Franklin's humiliation.

VI

For several years the dispute over Parliament's right to
levy taxes in the colonies had been dormant. Only the
tax on tea remained on the books, but this was a moot
point, since the colonies refused to import it. This created a serious financial problem for the British East India Company, which had a large surplus. At its urging,
Parliament passed the Tea Act in May 1773 in order to
create an American market for tea. This act eliminated
British duties on tea being transshipped to America,
thereby reducing its cost to American consumers.
The act, however, did not eliminate the duties that
the American colonists would have to pay and hence
was regarded by them as an attack on the autonomy
of colonial legislatures. Lord North, the prime minister, appears to have been insensitive rather than confrontational; at the same time the Tea Act was passed,
he was rebuffing a French attempt at better relations.
This was hardly the act of someone anticipating a crisis
in America in which the French might be tempted to
intervene.[28]

A few days before the hearing in the Cockpit, news
reached London that some 350 chests of tea had been
taken from a ship and dumped in Boston Harbor by a
group of men dressed as American Indians. The news
provoked general outrage and undoubtedly contributed

to the severity of the tongue-lashing administered to
Franklin. At the end of March 1774, George III signed
the Boston Port Act, just passed by Parliament. This
act closed the port of Boston to most shipping until
the East India Company was recompensed. Franklin,
already in disgrace, could do little to prevent passage
of the bill. He signed a petition protesting the injustice of penalizing all the citizens of Massachusetts
for an act caused by "persons unknown," but he also
wrote to Massachusetts urging the legislature to offer
satisfaction to the East India Company. Moreover, he
wrote a letter to a London newspaper, the *Public Advertiser*, maintaining that all Americans agreed they were
subject to the king, even if not everyone felt the same
about Parliament.[29]

Parliament did not stop with punishing Boston.
On May 20 the king signed two further acts abolishing self-government for Massachusetts and transfer-
ring direct legislative and judicial power to the Crown.
Franklin, finally disabused of his illusions about royal
government, warned the Pennsylvania Assembly to exercise prudence, since nothing could protect it from
the same fate. He signed another petition and lobbied
members of the House of Commons against the acts,
but again he was helpless to prevent their passage.
Anonymously he submitted a bitterly satirical letter
to the *Public Advertiser* proposing that Parliament pass
a bill authorizing the British army to castrate all the
males in North America. To his son, the governor of
New Jersey, he recommended that Americans adopt a
new trade embargo.[30] In September 1774 the American

colonies convened a Continental Congress in order to petition the king and take whatever measures might be necessary.

Hopeless to prevent further "Coercive Acts" against America, Franklin seemed destined to remain a bystander. Instead, members of the British government who were concerned about the deteriorating situation turned to him as a potential peacemaker. They believed he had power to negotiate on behalf of the colonies; Franklin did not, but he was willing to make suggestions. After the discussions failed and Franklin was aboard the ship that took him back to America, he began a lengthy description of them in the form of a letter to his son that is our main source for what happened.[31]

The identity of the British ministers involved is still a mystery. The first person to seek Franklin's help in arranging a compromise settlement was not a member of the present government, however, but the great William Pitt, now Earl of Chatham. Franklin had been hoping to meet him ever since his first mission. At the end of August 1774, he finally was invited by Chatham to his estate to discuss American affairs; Franklin reassured him that Americans were not intent on independence. Franklin also consulted with a mutual friend, another prominent member of the parliamentary opposition, Charles Pratt, Baron Camden. Negotiations with the current British government did not start until December. We know that they were sanctioned by William Legge, Earl of Dartmouth, the secretary of state for the colonies, but other government officials may also have been involved, including Prime Minister North. There were two different sets of intermediaries. They first contacted Franklin separately, but were in communication with each other. The first set consisted of two prominent Quakers whom Franklin knew well, the wealthy banker and merchant David Barclay and the physician John Fothergill, whose patients included both Franklin and Dartmouth. Barclay and Fothergill in turn introduced Franklin to another of Fothergill's patients, Thomas Villiers, Baron Hyde, a member of the Privy Council. Franklin was not aware of all of Barclay and Fothergill's negotiations with the government. The other set of intermediaries consisted of the Honorable Caroline Howe, who invited Franklin to play chess with her, and her brother Rear Adm. Viscount Richard Howe, to whom she introduced her new chess partner. After encouragement from both Lady Howe and Fothergill, Franklin on December 6 gave the two Quakers a set of seventeen "hints" about terms that might produce a reconciliation. These hints, which they forwarded to Dartmouth, included a suggestion that Americans would pay for the tea if the British government repealed the Coercive Acts. (Eventually Franklin offered to advance personally the money to pay for the tea in the hope that Boston would repay him.) Franklin also indicated that American assemblies would agree to the Navigation Acts (restricting British American trade to British and British American ships and crews), as well as to providing financial aid to the Crown in case of war. Parliament, however, would have to renounce its supposed rights to tax the colonies and to enact internal legislation for them. In late December Admiral Howe, who had received from Barclay a copy of the hints, urged Franklin to soften the terms. Instead, Franklin asked the British government to withdraw its troops and fleet from Boston and to authorize the meeting of an American congress to discuss terms of agreement, the first Continental Congress having already been adjourned.

English public opinion was so opposed to America that Parliament hardly would have agreed to the terms offered by Franklin. It buried in committee a petition from the Continental Congress first presented by Franklin and two other Massachusetts colonial agents to the king. Moreover, the House of Lords soundly defeated Chatham's proposals for a compromise peace. Franklin, with whom Chatham had consulted, was in attendance for the February 1 debate, during which John Montagu, Earl of Sandwich, the First Lord of the Admiralty, referred to him as one of the bitterest and most mischievous enemies Britain had ever known.[32]

During the negotiations Franklin had indignantly rejected hints of a personal reward from the British government if he brokered a peace. He responded with similar anger to threats, such as the danger to American seaports if a settlement wasn't reached. He responded that the British were welcome to make bonfires with his houses in Philadelphia and Boston, but warned that the British eventually would have to pay with interest for whatever damage they did. Any compromise that did not resolve underlying differences was worse than pointless because, as Franklin stated, those who surrender essential liberty in order to obtain temporary safety deserve neither.[33]

In February 1775 Franklin learned of the death of his wife. With his well developed capacity for self-delusion, he apparently had been able to ignore the warning signs in her letters of her deteriorating health. He had postponed returning to Philadelphia as she had begged.[34] Her death now gave him an excuse to leave, although he did promise to wait for Lord Howe if the latter were appointed by the government as a commissioner to negotiate with the colonists. This not yet happening, Franklin sailed for America; on March 22, while aboard ship, he began his journal of the recent negotiations.

Franklin's feelings seem to have been a mixture of sadness and rage. His friend Joseph Priestley, the great scientist, read American newspapers with him on the day before his departure from London and later described him as having been in tears. Franklin told Arthur Lee, his replacement as colonial agent, that he might be back in England in the autumn. This was unrealistic, as an arrest order soon was issued against him for leaving the country while a lawsuit (in the Hutchinson letters incident) was pending. He composed a bitter letter to Dartmouth calling for Britain to make reparations for the financial harm it had done to Boston, but friends, fearing for his safety, persuaded him not to send it.[35] When he arrived in America, he found himself in a revolution where there was more room for anger than for sadness.

Chapter Three

Eighteen Months in Congress

I

BECAUSE WE KNOW the outcome of the American Revolution, it is difficult for us to appreciate how unlikely was its success. By all odds the highly professional British army and navy should have suppressed the rebellion in America, as they had defeated uprisings in Ireland and Scotland and would defeat uprisings in Canada and India. Parliament was virtually united against the rebels, and British public opinion almost as much so. Only once had Americans defeated a European army (at Louisbourg in 1745). The northern and southern colonies had little history of military cooperation, and many Americans remained loyal to the Crown. Franklin's experience in the Cockpit surely must have been a clear demonstration that he could expect little mercy if he aided armed resistance. Why did he and the other rebel leaders risk their very lives?

It seems clear that they came to feel that they had no choice, Franklin with his greater experience of the British government sooner than most. The British government menaced their ability to choose how and by whom they would be governed. Their property and perhaps even their religion would be at the disposal of those who viewed them with contempt. Some

Americans, particularly those who feared the lower class, were afraid to resist or felt resistance unnecessary. Most, however, eventually chose rebellion and war over submission to Britons who wounded their pride, menaced their self-interest, and mocked their ideals.

Franklin was en route to America when the Battles of Lexington and Concord took place. He did not learn of them until his arrival more than two weeks later. His return to Philadelphia on May 5, however, was fortunately timed. A new Continental Congress was to convene in five days, and the Pennsylvania Assembly immediately expanded the delegation that it had appointed so as to include him. He accepted without hesitation, knowing better than most the risks involved. He proved far more radical than the cautious Pennsylvania Assembly probably expected. As late as May 1776, the assembly and most of the Pennsylvania delegation in Congress were still opposed to declaring independence.[1]

Shortly after his return to Philadelphia, Franklin began meeting with his political protégé, Joseph Galloway, and with his son, William, still governor of New Jersey.[2] At one of the meetings Franklin indicated his support for America's moving toward independence, but his son and Galloway disagreed. Franklin soon broke off relations with Galloway, but he could not give up on his own son so easily. There was now a new bond between them. Franklin had brought back with him from London William's 15-year-old illegitimate son, William Temple Franklin, who accompanied his father to New Jersey but remained in close contact with his grandfather.[3]

Franklin at first was more guarded with others about his political views; some, indeed, initially suspected him of being a British spy. Franklin eventually dispersed such suspicions by the range of his patriotic activities, not only in Congress but also as postmaster general, president of the Pennsylvania Committee of Safety, and president of the Pennsylvania Constitutional Convention. He was also elected to the Pennsylvania Assembly and the Philadelphia Committee of Inspection and Observation, but lacked the time for them because of the demands of his service in the Continental Congress. Before Congress adjourned on August 1, 1775, for a six-week recess, it had appointed Franklin to committees dealing with the postal service, the drafting of a petition to the king, the manufacture of saltpeter, the issuance of paper currency, the drafting of a declaration of the cause for taking up arms, the protection of American trade, the supervision of Indian affairs, the consideration of a resolution sent by Lord North, and the manufacture of lead.[4]

The list of committees on which Franklin served indicates the dual nature of the task faced by Congress. On the one hand, it had to explore the possibility of negotiating a peaceful resolution to the dispute with Great Britain, a dispute that was becoming a full-scale war that few Americans wished. On the other, it had to create national institutions in order to coordinate the efforts of thirteen hitherto separate colonies to defend themselves.

With the British government unwilling to back down, the only hope for a negotiated settlement was through economic pressure, as had been successful in the past; should that fail, America would have to defend itself. Shortly after his return to America, Franklin wrote that he expected non-importation (already in effect) and non-exportation (due to come into effect in September) to end the controversy, but that he believed it absolutely necessary to be prepared to repel force by force. He advised the Moravians, a reputedly pacifist sect like the Quakers, to conciliate those who resented them by permitting their members who wished to take military training to do so. A letter to a friend in England, however, betrays his sadness and pessimism. He wrote that he thought it unlikely he would live long enough to see England again or to see an end to the civil war begun by General Gage (who had sent troops to Lexington and Concord).[5]

There is a dramatic change in tone in Franklin's letters after the Battle of Bunker Hill on June 17. He was outraged by the British destruction of the nearby town of Charlestown before the battle, a seeming confirmation of British threats to burn American seaports. He drafted, but did not send, a letter to his publisher, William Strahan, a member of the House of Commons, in which he said Strahan's hands were stained with the blood of Franklin's relatives and claimed they now were enemies. To the American sympathizer Joseph Priestley, he described the British government as a combination of "robbery, murder, famine, fire and pestilence." He wrote John Sargent, his English banker, that most of his American property consisted of houses in seaport towns that the British government had begun to burn; he supposed it wicked enough to burn them all. He enclosed a list of British atrocities with a letter to his close friend Bishop Jonathan Shipley, including not only the burning of Charlestown but also the encouragement of slaves and Indians to murder innocent people. A common theme of these letters is Franklin's horror at the death of civilians, particularly women and children. This remained a concern of his; after the war he attempted to provide in various treaties for the future protection of noncombatants.[6]

He warned both Priestley and Sargent that the British had one more opportunity to save their connection with America but that it probably would be the last. This was a reference to Congress's Olive Branch petition professing loyalty to the king and asking redress. Although Franklin was on the committee to prepare it, the more moderate John Dickinson drafted it. Carried to England by Thomas Penn's nephew Richard, it was rebuffed with less ceremony than had been the petition of the first Continental Congress, which at least the king had forwarded to Parliament. As Franklin surely expected, the new petition was not even accepted.[7]

Before Congress adjourned, Franklin suggested that it offer an annual payment of £100,000 if Britain would make peace and give Americans the same privileges as Scotland. The proposal made little impact on his fellow delegates. He also circulated a suggestion that was more realistic—articles of confederation for "The United Colonies of North America."[8] He would

have to wait awhile before his colleagues were ready
for such a complete break from Britain.

II

The Battle of Bunker Hill purchased time for America to organize its defenses, because it prevented the
British army from breaking out of Boston, which was
connected to the rest of Massachusetts only by a nar-
row neck of land. The British army did not immediately receive reinforcements to replace its heavy losses
during the battle. Moreover, not until August 23 did
George III proclaim the colonies in a state of rebellion.
It took until the following summer to place the British army on a wartime footing, partly by hiring professional troops from several German principalities.
Nonetheless the Americans faced enormous obstacles
in organizing a defense against an excellent army and
the world's greatest navy. Virtually everything had to
be improvised. Even George Washington, who proved a
forceful leader for the army, never had fought European regular troops (although some of his subordinates
like Horatio Gates and Charles Lee were veterans of the
British army). The army, moreover, lacked engineer-
ing and artillery officers, who normally had extensive
practical training; the artillery service had to be placed
under the command of a talented amateur, Henry
Knox. Almost miraculously Washington received cannon with which to fight. The British failed to reinforce
or evacuate the huge fortress of Fort Ticonderoga on
Lake Champlain, whose small garrison was surprised
and captured by Ethan Allen's group of irregulars, the

Green Mountain Boys, on May 10, 1775. Over the winter of 1775–76, about sixty of its cannon were transported by sled to the American forces besieging Boston.

Everything else was in short supply, as Franklin soon learned. During August and early September of 1775 Congress was in recess, and he was the only delegate left in Philadelphia. He was very busy, though, as chairman of the Pennsylvania Committee of Safety. He dispatched all the spare gunpowder in Philadelphia, 2,400 pounds worth, to Maj. Gen. Philip Schuyler, commanding the American army in northern New York; in exchange he asked Schuyler to send lead to Philadelphia. The New York Provincial Congress, fearing an attack on New York City, also begged for gunpowder. Franklin, having just received some, ordered a ton to be sent, although it was returned when an alternate source turned up. (Washington's army besieging Boston also was busy collecting gunpowder.)

Gunpowder was not the only thing in short supply. The shortage of muskets was so acute that Franklin designed a pike, a fourteen-foot pole made of pine with an eighteen-inch spear at its end, for use by the Pennsylvania volunteers; the following February he argued to Gen. Charles Lee the usefulness not only of pikes but also of bows and arrows. In compensation for his busy schedule providing for arms, Franklin had a respite from attending Congress. Prior to the adjournment he had met with the Pennsylvania Committee of Safety from 6 to 9 a.m. before spending a full day in Congress. He later said that he had spent twelve hours a day on public business. It is hardly surprising that, as John Adams remembered, Franklin sometimes fell asleep in his chair.[9]

One of the first orders of business for Congress when it reconvened in mid-September was the appointment of what it named the Secret Committee, charged with obtaining arms and ammunition. It paid tribute to Franklin's business acumen by appointing him as one of the nine original members. The export of American produce, otherwise forbidden by the non-exportation agreement, was authorized if it were in exchange for war materiel. Many war supplies such as gunpowder were smuggled from Europe or the Caribbean, often through the Dutch West Indian island of St. Eustatius; tracing this trade is as difficult as tracing today's trade in illegal drugs. Another source of munitions was by capture. George Washington enjoyed some success fitting out a number of small schooners to intercept supply ships carrying food and munitions to the besieged garrison in Boston.[10]

The British navy was unsuccessful in cutting off the supply of munitions. It failed to provide enough ships to blockade the American coast, a difficult task in any case and one that became more difficult in 1776 when numerous warships were needed to support the landing and supply of a huge British army. Part of the reason for the British failure was fear of the French navy. This led the British to partially man some larger ships instead of spreading the navy's supply of sailors among many small ships. Another important cause of failure was the desire of the British government to spend as little money as it could in winning the war, not the last time in the history of warfare that this happened. A surge of British ships blockading the American coast came far too late; only in 1782, with the results of the war largely determined, did the British successfully choke off American seaborne trade.[11]

As challenging as finding munitions was the problem of turning minutemen and other militia into professional soldiers. On September 21, 1775, Washington, seeing his troops short of money and supplies and his army on the verge of disintegration, wrote to Congress for help. Again Congress turned to Franklin, already involved in raising and organizing Pennsylvania troops, as he had during the two previous wars. It named him and his fellow delegates Thomas Lynch and Benjamin Harrison as a committee to travel to Cambridge, Massachusetts, to meet with Washington and representatives from Connecticut, Rhode Island, and Massachusetts. Franklin, named chairman of the committee, and the others were in Cambridge from October 15 through October 24, 1776. They advised Washington about the proper size of the army, the salaries of enlisted men, the proper daily food allowance, the type of muskets to be used, the articles of war to be followed and the punishments for their violation, the treatment of prisoners, and a variety of other topics. Upon returning to Philadelphia they offered advice on pay and enlistments for Washington's army and reported the destruction of another seaport by the British, Falmouth (now Portland, Maine). Soon thereafter the *Boston Gazette* published a satirical drinking song, "The King's Own Regulars," that Franklin later admitted having written. The editors of the Franklin Papers make the guess that it was written in Cambridge after work was done. As a litany of British military disasters from 1745 to 1775, it reminded its audience that, although the new American army had its problems, the enemy that it faced was far from invincible.[12]

III

While Franklin was returning to Philadelphia, he was reelected to Congress.[13] Franklin and his committee reported what was needed by Washington's army, but unless supplies were found, their recommendations would be academic. Some in Congress like John Adams felt an ambassador should be sent to France to ask for assistance, but as yet there was not a majority for taking so drastic a step. Instead, at the end of November 1776, Congress voted to establish the Committee of Secret Correspondence to communicate with American sympathizers in England and on the European continent. Franklin, the New York delegate John Jay, and three others were named to the committee.

The committee quickly wrote to Arthur Lee, Franklin's successor as Massachusetts agent in London. Franklin then wrote on the committee's behalf to ask his friend in the Netherlands, Charles-Guillaume Frédéric Dumas, what courts in Europe might be well disposed toward the American cause. Specifically, as Franklin explained to Dumas, it wished to know what courts might make a commercial alliance should the Americans declare their independence. He informed Dumas about American shortages of arms and ammunition and asked him to hire two engineers for the American army.[14]

Long before the letters could reach Europe, a foreign court made contact with the committee. First, however, there was a false contact. Pierre Penet and Emmanuel de Pliarne, two merchants from the wealthy French colony of St. Domingue (now Haiti), arrived in Rhode Island on December 10 with an offer to supply the Americans with weapons. Their way was paid to Philadelphia, where they deceived the Secret Committee into thinking they had been sent by the French government. The committee provided them with a list of supplies needed in America which Penet then delivered to the French government on May 5, 1776. Almost simultaneously with Penet and Pliarne's arrival in Philadelphia, a young man named Julien-Alexandre Achard de Bonvouloir came from the West Indies. He met several times in Carpenters' Hall with the Committee of Secret Correspondence. He offered his personal services and told the committee that he believed France was well disposed toward the colonies. He also volunteered to carry a message to France. Unlike the other visitors, he was much more than he claimed, for he had been sent to Philadelphia on the orders of Charles Gravier, comte de Vergennes, the foreign minister of France.

Vergennes eventually became a vital presence in the life of Franklin and was indispensable to the success of the American Revolution.[15] Franklin correctly placed his trust in Vergennes's determination to see America independent, but neither he nor any other American had a clue as to what motivated him. The key to understanding

Vergennes is his lengthy service in the Secret du Roi, a group of diplomats selected by King Louis XV to work in secret for the election of a French candidate to the throne of Poland, an elective monarchy. The Secret du Roi gradually took on a life of its own, becoming the most important part of Vergennes' public life and hence critical to the French decision to intervene in the American Revolution. Because France's chief rival in Poland was Russia, the Secret du Roi became the chief instrument of those Frenchmen who feared that Russian ambitions in eastern Europe would undermine France's relations with Poland and the other powers of eastern Europe, Sweden, and the Ottoman Empire (consisting not only of Turkey but much of the Balkans). In 1772 the Russians along with Poland's other neighbors, Prussia and Austria, grabbed huge slices of Poland for themselves without even warning France. Vergennes, still a member of the Secret du Roi, was the French minister in Stockholm at the time. He became convinced that the key to stopping Russia was to weaken its supporter, Britain. He finally was given the chance. Louis XV died in 1774 and was succeeded by his young grandson, the idealistic and naïve Louis XVI. Wishing to remain at peace, Louis rejected naming the head of the Secret du Roi as foreign minister and instead picked Vergennes, who had a reputation for caution. He did not realize that Vergennes was violently anti-Russian, as were his two undersecretaries, the brothers Conrad-Alexandre and Joseph-Mathias Gérard, who had long experience in Polish affairs. (Franklin later would have extensive dealings with both brothers, although he does not seem to have been acquainted with their backgrounds.) Vergennes was prepared to do whatever was necessary to weaken Britain, even if it meant deceiving Louis. His first step was ordering Bonvouloir to Philadelphia.

Franklin and his colleagues were astute enough to realize the opportunity presented by Bonvouloir. They requested that he send them three pieces of information: whether the French court was well disposed toward them, what they had to do to obtain two army engineers, and whether American ships could come to French ports to trade American produce for arms. Bonvouloir expressed his personal belief that France wished them well and could provide two engineers or even more. If the Americans were willing to risk British interception, he believed they would meet no obstacles in trading directly with France.[16]

Vergennes received Bonvouloir's report on February 27, 1776. It sparked a debate that would have enormous consequences for Benjamin Franklin and for the American Revolution. Congress was too impatient to wait, however. It voted to send to France Silas Deane, a Connecticut merchant and former congressional delegate. On March 2 Franklin drafted (on behalf of the Committee of Secret Correspondence) Deane's instructions, including orders to seek an audience with Vergennes; two weeks earlier Franklin, this time as a member of the Secret Committee, had signed a contract advancing $200,000 to him and several business associates to purchase produce to be exchanged for cargoes in Europe.[17] Meanwhile, Franklin was preparing for a journey of his own.

IV

In June 1775 Congress had authorized the invasion of Canada. There was some military justification for the invasion. If successful, it would deprive the British of an invasion route into the American colonies. Its main justification, however, seems to have been ideological. As Americans were fighting for freedom, it seemed logical to help others fight for their freedom, too. They expected the Canadians to welcome them because they were fighting the British army, which fifteen years earlier had conquered Canada. Believing in the righteousness of their cause, the Americans failed to consider that the Canadians had reason to distrust them. There was a long history of animosity between Americans and Canadians. More important, the bulk of Canadians were Catholics, and the American army consisted mostly of Protestants. Thus the Americans chose to spread democracy by force, invade another country for its own good, and disregard the religious beliefs of those they were attempting to liberate. The results were disastrous. An American army commanded by Brig. Gen. Richard Montgomery (replacing Schuyler, who was in ill health) advanced into Canada, captured Montreal, and then rendezvoused near the fortified city of Quebec with a detachment from Washington's army under the command of Brig. Gen. Benedict Arnold. On December 31, 1775, Montgomery and Arnold attacked the city, but they were defeated and Montgomery was killed. The American army then settled down to besiege the city.[18]

In the middle of February 1776, a native of Montreal arrived in Philadelphia and conferred with the Committee of Secret Correspondence. He reported that the natives of Canada were unsure of which side to support. He asked Congress to send representatives to them to explain the nature of its dispute with Britain and to reassure them that the Americans wished only to put them in full possession of their liberty and then to enjoy friendship and union with them. As soon as Congress received the report of the committee on its meeting, it voted to send three delegates to Canada: Franklin, Samuel Chase of New York, and the prominent Roman Catholic Charles Carroll of Maryland. The delegation was accompanied by Carroll's cousin John, a Catholic priest who after the war became, with Franklin's recommendation, the head of Catholic missions in America and later the first Catholic bishop in the United States.

This mission was far more dangerous and demanding than Franklin's leisurely trip to Cambridge the previous autumn. Franklin was now 70, seriously overweight, and unused to physical hardship. He had to make a lengthy journey on bad roads in late winter to upstate New York and Canada, where he entered a combat zone. The journey from Philadelphia to Montreal took from March 26 until April 29. By the time Franklin reached Saratoga he began to fear that the fatigue of the journey would kill him, and he wrote to friends to say farewell. During the final stages of the journey the party had to contend with ice on Lake Champlain and with primitive conditions thereafter; for two days they had to sleep on bare floors in a pillaged house. When the delegates reached Montreal they discovered that the American army had no money to pay its bills. Pressed by creditors, they wrote Congress for money. On May 10 they learned that a small British squadron carrying reinforcements had just broken the American siege of Quebec. The American army that had been besieging the city was in full retreat and, moreover, had been stricken by a smallpox epidemic. The commissioners decided to send Father Carroll and the ailing Franklin back to report to Congress. They left Montreal the following day, and on May 30 Franklin was back in Philadelphia. Although Franklin's mission was a failure, he had demonstrated dramatically his dedication and courage.[19]

Twelve days after Franklin's return he was appointed to a congressional committee to draft a declaration of independence. Public opinion had shifted in favor of independence largely as a result of the pamphlet *Common Sense* by Thomas Paine, who had emigrated to Pennsylvania in late 1774 with a letter of introduction from Franklin to his son-in-law, Richard Bache. Franklin's correspondence contains only a brief mention of the pamphlet; in a later letter to Gen. Charles Lee introducing Paine, he described it as having made a great impression. Franklin did not commit to paper much discussion of his own political views during the months prior to the declaration, doubtless because he was so busy. Indeed, the press of congressional business forced him to resign on February 26 from the Pennsylvania Assembly and Committee of Safety; during the first half of 1776 he helped provide designs for continental currency and was appointed to eight new committees as well as undertaking the futile mission to Canada. There can be no doubt of his opinion, however. In a congressional debate on authorizing privateering, he suggested a declaration of war against Britain and prepared a resolution calling the British government violators of the commandments of God and all the principles of right and justice natural to man. His private correspondence, although sparse, was equally bitter. Hence he had absolutely no differences of opinion with either Thomas Jefferson, who wrote the Declaration of Independence, or John Adams, who like Franklin made a few suggestions to Jefferson. Perhaps it is fortunate that the others left the drafting to Jefferson; Adams was prone to verbosity, and Franklin had difficulty in controlling his rage against George III.[20]

The Declaration of Independence represented an important step in the Pennsylvania revolution as well as the American. The assembly was dominated by conservatives, and on July 1 the Pennsylvania delegation in Congress that it had selected was one of only two voting against independence (Franklin being outvoted by his colleagues). The following day it finally voted with the others. Unsurprisingly the Pennsylvania radicals decided to replace the assembly with a more democratic body. From the middle of July to the end of September, Pennsylvania was governed by a constitutional convention meeting in the same building as the Continental Congress. It unanimously elected Franklin its president. The constitution that it drafted was

the most democratic of any of the new state constitutions. It incorporated some of Franklin's ideas such as
a unicameral legislature.[21] Just as it was completing its
work, news arrived from Europe that soon gave Franklin a new set of responsibilities.

v

Silas Deane took three months to reach France. He spent
a month in Bordeaux before traveling to Paris, where
he arrived on July 6. Much had happened in France
during his voyage. The arrival of Bonvouloir's report
presented Vergennes with the opportunity of weakening Britain. He knew that if the Americans achieved
their independence, Britain would lose its monopoly
of American trade. Not only would France profit from
gaining a share of this trade, but more importantly he
believed that the loss of American trade would seriously weaken the British economy and hence its ability to finance its own wars and those of its friends like
Russia. If America obtained its independence through
French clandestine aid without France's having to go
to war, so much the better, but Vergennes was prepared to fight in order to restore the position France
had lost in the European balance of power. Far from
hating Britain, he was anxious that once it had been
humbled Britain would join with France in protecting
Europe from expansionist powers like Russia.

The challenge for Vergennes was that such a pre-
ventive war was directly contrary to Louis XVI's pro-
fessed goals of avoiding war and serving his people's
well-being. Fortunately for Vergennes, if unfortunately

for France, the king was extraordinarily gullible. Vergennes argued that it would be prudent for France to take actions to prolong the American rebellion at least a year so it could put its colonies in a state of defense; if the American revolt was successful, the British might seek compensation by attacking French or Spanish colonies in the West Indies. The king then called for all the members of his council of state, his chief advisory body, to present their opinions.

The responses were presented in early April 1776. Vergennes' new arguments were drafted for him by his undersecretary, Joseph-Mathias Gérard, a skilled writer who a few years earlier had translated into French an English satire on the partition of Poland. His memoir for Vergennes directly presented the case for assisting America to gain its independence: a war between Britain and France was inevitable, and American independence would harm British trade and weaken Britain in the balance of power. Only one minister dared to disagree: Anne-Robert-Jacques Turgot, the French controller general of finances (finance minister). Turgot challenged Vergennes' basic premises. He argued that the chief danger facing Louis was the state of his finances, which needed a continuation of peace to improve. He also argued that France would actually profit from a British victory because such a victory would be very expensive to Britain, and moreover that an American victory would not seriously harm the British economy. Turgot was correct on all these points, but on May 2 the king decided in favor of Vergennes, and ten days later he dismissed Turgot from office. Louis decided to provide secretly the Americans arms worth 1 million *livres*, equivalent to perhaps $5 million in today's terms. To shield the French government's involvement, they were provided at cost to a trading company that in turn sold them to the Americans in exchange for promises of shipments of tobacco. The company, soon named Roderigue Hortalez and Company, was headed by the businessman and playwright Pierre-Augustin Caron de Beaumarchais, whom Vergennes knew from his work on behalf of the Secret du Roi. At the same time, the king decided for precautionary reasons to arm a few ships of the French navy. Again the king was deceived. The French naval minister was the highly capable Antoine-Raymond-Gualbert-Gabriel de Sartine, previously the chief administrator of Paris and head of the Paris police. He, too, was a former member of the Secret du Roi and Vergennes' close political ally. He now began secretly to prepare the French navy for war, disregarding all budgetary limits.[22]

Meanwhile Congress rebuffed peace feelers from the British. On September 9–11, 1776, Franklin, Edward Rutledge, and John Adams traveled from Philadelphia to Staten Island to meet with Adm. Richard Howe and his brother, Gen. William Howe. After the evacuation of Boston, the British had shifted the main theater of military operations to New York. They landed a huge army on Staten Island and then invaded Long Island, winning a great victory over Washington's army at Brooklyn Heights on August 27. General Howe and his brother, who commanded the accompanying fleet, were not only the chief British military officers in

America but also had been named peace commissioners charged with negotiating a settlement with the Continental Congress. Upon their invitation, Congress sent three commissioners of its own to meet with them. Only the admiral was present, as the general was with his army; he had no authority, however, to negotiate with Congress and could only confer with the American delegates as private gentlemen, which proved pointless. They took leave of him and returned to Philadelphia.

There are several ironies to the meeting at Staten Island. The most poignant is that during their peace discussions in 1774–75 Adm. Richard Howe had hoped that he would be selected to go to America to negotiate peace and that Franklin would accompany him; instead, Franklin was now on the opposite side, with the two having irreconcilable differences. The second irony is the identity of Howe's secretary who took minutes of the meeting. He was Henry Strachey, who would be a member of a far different and more successful British peace delegation in 1782. The third is more amusing. During their trip Franklin and his friend Adams had a disagreement about whether or not to sleep with the windows open, Franklin being a fanatical advocate of the advantages of fresh air. In coming years, Franklin and Adams would be thrown together again in Paris, only with far more serious disagreements, this time on how to deal with the French.[23]

VI

Just as Franklin and his colleagues returned from Staten Island, Congress received exciting news from

61

Jacques Barbeu-Dubourg, the editor of the French edition of Franklin's writings. He had accompanied Pierre Penet to his meeting with Vergennes, three days after the king's decision to aid the American rebels. Penet's list of the military supplies needed in America was opportune, and Barbeu-Dubourg briefly had hopes of heading the supply effort before Beaumarchais was selected instead. His lengthy letter of June 10–July 2, 1776, reported to Franklin the sale of war materiel from French arsenals and the impending departure for America of needed artillery officers; a short note of July 5 falsely reported France readying for war. The former letter (perhaps accompanied by the latter) seems to have reached Philadelphia in mid-September and apparently was the impetus for Congress to expand the American presence in France to three equal members with each having the title of commissioner. The commissioners inherited a mission to perform for Congress. On July 18 a congressional committee had submitted a draft commercial treaty to be submitted to the French government; Franklin called John Adams's attention to articles in a book of treaties, which Adams then incorporated into the draft treaty he prepared for the committee. The committee was expanded on August 27 and ordered to draft instructions for negotiating the treaty. Matters proceeded rapidly. The committee reported to Congress on September 10. A week later Congress approved the draft treaty, and on the 24th it approved the instructions.

By now Congress had received Dubourg's letter. It elected Franklin, Deane, and Thomas Jefferson as commissioners. When Jefferson turned down the appointment, a fellow Virginian, Arthur Lee, was selected as his replacement. Lee, formerly Franklin's successor as agent for the Massachusetts Assembly, was still in England and could easily travel to France.[24]

The draft treaty and instructions reveal Congress's reluctance to become involved in European diplomacy; in *Common Sense* Paine had blamed the English monarchy for America's unnecessary involvement in European wars, and Adams felt the same repugnance for foreign wars. These new documents also greatly overestimated the importance of American trade. France was expected to provide convoy protection for American ships, to provide weapons, to sell or lend the United States eight ships of the line (the largest warships of the day), and to sign a commercial treaty. Any of these actions would cause Britain to declare war on France, but Congress did not promise assistance to France in case of such a war. Instead the commissioners could only promise to provide no aid to Britain, to give France prior notice of an American-British peace treaty, and to offer Britain no exclusive trade privileges when peace was signed.[25] This lack of reciprocity was naïve and arrogant; France would sign no commercial treaty without a military alliance, and it would sign neither treaty until its naval rearmament was sufficiently advanced that the French navy could hope for victory.

By late October Congress found a ship to carry Franklin to France, the brig *Reprisal*, commanded by Lambert Wickes, one of the best ship captains in the new Continental (American) navy.[26] This time, however,

Franklin would not be accompanied by his son William, who had refused to abandon his responsibilities as royal governor of New Jersey. He had been removed from office in June 1776 and was now under house arrest in New Jersey. His father did nothing to help him, although he did send $60 (i.e., dollars backed by specie, equivalent to several thousand contemporary dollars) to his ailing daughter-in-law, left behind in New Jersey. (Her sister-in-law, Sally Franklin Bache, ever generous, invited her to Philadelphia, but she was afraid of leaving her house to looters.)[27] William Franklin also lost the battle for the affections of his teenage son, William Temple Franklin, who accompanied his grandfather on the *Reprisal*. Also aboard was 8-year-old Benjamin Franklin Bache, sent to Europe by Sally and her husband, Richard, for his education. Franklin and his grandsons sailed from Philadelphia on October 27. Franklin had risked his life traveling to Canada the previous spring. Now he risked both capture by the British and the terrible weather of the North Atlantic; on its return voyage to America the following autumn the *Reprisal* would be lost in a storm with all but one of her crew. During the voyage Franklin suffered greatly, particularly from the unsatisfactory food, but fortunately the *Reprisal* met no British warships and enjoyed a quick though stormy passage. On December 3 the Franklin party was rowed ashore to the little French port of Auray.[28]

Chapter Four

Franklin and the French

I

FRANKLIN AND HIS GRANDSONS slowly made their way to Paris. In several ways he differed from the other members of the diplomatic corps who attended the French court, which usually was located at the royal chateau of Versailles, a few miles from Paris.[1] To begin with, at age 70 he was exceptionally old for someone beginning a diplomatic career, and he was frequently in ill health, particularly from gout and kidney or bladder stones. His preparation for that career, his service as a colonial agent was as good a training, however, as was received by most diplomats. Many of them, like Vergennes, began as embassy officials, often serving in a secretarial capacity. Franklin had learned the workings of the British court firsthand; it had taught him patience, skepticism, and the necessity of prudence and tact. There were gaps in his education, however, that no one in Congress could help him overcome. Unlike European diplomats, he did not receive formal instruction about the history and politics of the court to which he was being sent. This was a serious problem for Franklin and his fellow diplomats. Both Franklin and John Adams, who joined the American commission in 1778, tried to learn European diplomacy by reading books of treaties, but their knowledge was superficial. Had Franklin had any knowledge of the long-standing French suspicion of Russia, for example, he could have made a stronger case in 1781 against sending Francis Dana on an unsolicited mission to St. Petersburg.[2] Because of his inadequate training, Franklin probably was not the equal of the best European diplomats (for example, George Adam Graf von Starhemberg, the Austrian ambassador to the French court during the previous war). Vergennes, however, considered him wise and conciliatory, even if aged and indolent; in contrast, he described John Jay, Franklin's colleague from 1782 to 1784, as egotistical, prejudiced, and ill-humored.[3]

In addition to his being aged and uninformed about European diplomacy, Franklin's social status and wealth were considerably inferior to those of a typical European diplomat. Franklin, however, was able to turn his not being of noble birth to his advantage by letting people think he was a benevolent Quaker. Even his usual shortage of funds did not have a serious social impact. Diplomats were expected to entertain lavishly, usually from their own funds, but until 1783, representatives of other countries were forbidden to officially meet with Franklin. Until the British government officially recognized American independence, representatives of the United States were accredited only by France (and, after 1782, by the Netherlands). This at least saved them from having to host expensive entertainments. Franklin did manage to hold weekly dinners for his fellow Americans in Paris as well as occasional parties, like celebrations of the Fourth of July.

Franklin compensated for his lack of social standing by tapping into several social networks. One was the scientific community, particularly members of the Académie royale des sciences and the Société royale de médecine. At their meetings Franklin encountered and often befriended aristocrats, such as the great chemist Antoine-Laurent Lavoisier. Perhaps even more important were Franklin's Masonic contacts. He joined and later became vénérable (head official) of the most prestigious of all the French masonic lodges, the Neuf Soeurs, named after the Muses (or Nine Sisters). Franklin met other French aristocrats, such as the marquis de Lafayette, as a result of the rather naïve mania for the American cause among the French aristocracy, most of whom were strongly anti-British. Franklin became enormously popular among all sections of the French public, but he did not seek out the common people or those of dubious reputation. (He did meet with Voltaire, but there is no record of his having any contact with Denis Diderot, former chief editor of the suspect *Encyclopédie*.) Franklin's main challenge was that of not frightening the aristocracy, whose opinion mattered most at court.[4] His wit, charm, and good manners were indispensable. Thus he was the soothing public face of the American Revolution, somewhat like Premier Zhou Enlai for the Chinese Revolution or Peoples Commissar for Foreign Affairs Maxim Litvinov for the Russian Revolution.[5] Apparently he took particular care to avoid the rivals of Vergennes, like the duc de Choiseul, a former foreign minister. In return Vergennes provided Franklin with his two most important contacts. The first was Franklin's landlord, the wealthy arms contractor Jacques-Donatien Leray de Chaumont, who already had been providing Deane with gunpowder and saltpeter.[6] The other was the banker Rodolphe-Ferdinand Grand, whose brother Georges had helped Vergennes when he was French minister in Stockholm. Franklin occupied a wing of Chaumont's residence in the wealthy village of Passy, halfway between Paris and Versailles, where he met neighbors such as the Brillon family, who would become close friends. Mme Brillon, with whom Franklin engaged in a lengthy flirtation, was a talented musician, yet another entry for him into European society. Music was one of Franklin's greatest delights. Among his celebrated inventions was the armonica, an array of glass cylinders played by touch, for which Mozart, among others, composed; sadly, however, there is no indication Franklin attended the Paris concerts of the young touring musician.

Franklin's reputation as the greatest of all American diplomats is somewhat exaggerated. He neglected security. Sometimes he exceeded his instructions, such as by hinting to a British negotiator in 1782 that if Canada were ceded to the United States, Congress would indemnify Loyalists for the loss of their property.[7] Perhaps most dangerous for him, he undermined his support in Congress by not communicating with America more punctually. No American diplomat ever had a more critical mission, however. On balance Franklin performed it with great skill in spite of obstacles like lack of training and difficulties of communication that modern diplomats do not have to face. Certainly no other American of his day could have replaced him, just as no other American general could have replaced Washington. Both men had shortcomings, but these are of secondary importance, given what they were able to accomplish.

II

Franklin and his grandsons arrived in Paris on December 20, and Arthur Lee arrived two days later. Vergennes came to Paris a week later to meet secretly with Franklin, Lee, and Deane, who gave him a copy of Congress's proposed commercial agreement. On January 5, 1777, they sent him a memoir and letter, while also providing a copy of the memoir to the Spanish ambassador at the French court. The memoir castigated the "uncommon cruelty" of the British in burning American towns that winter and in instigating slave rebellions and Indian raids. It described the activities of Congress, but warned that the lack of markets for American trade might encourage defeatism. The letter asked for eight fully manned ships of the line, as well as muskets, bayonets, cannon, and ammunition.

The American request posed a problem for the French government. Because French naval rearmament was far from complete, an immediate war with Britain was certain to be disastrous. To avoid provoking the British government, France had suspended the departure for America of Beaumarchais' first munitions shipments, and for the same reason Vergennes was unwilling to meet publicly with the commissioners. Louis XVI thus refused the commissioners' request but agreed secretly to loan them 2 million *livres*. The news was delivered by Conrad-Alexandre Gérard, who henceforth served as Vergennes' liaison with the Americans. The commissioners in turn reassured Gérard that they had no intention of rushing the king into measures of which he disapproved and promised to follow his wishes. They received the first quarterly installment of the loan on January 17. Soon thereafter they received an advance of 1 million *livres* from the Farmers General, the consortium of bankers handling the French government's tobacco monopoly, on the promise of repayment in tobacco.[8]

French aid was restricted to financial payments in secret until almost the end of 1777, when naval rearmament was nearly finished and news from America gave Vergennes an excuse to pressure Louis XVI into a more active policy. Meanwhile the commissioners, rebuffed by Vergennes, generally refrained from pressuring him until late September, when their financial difficulties led them again to ask for assistance. Franklin's many months of waiting in the antechambers of British officials during his missions for the Pennsylvania Assembly proved good training for the long wait. To save money the commissioners sent Arthur Lee on missions to Spain and Prussia, but he was unwelcome at either court, and in Berlin his papers were stolen. Meanwhile Franklin remained in Passy and publicized the American cause in numerous ways. He helped the duc de La Rochefoucauld translate the American state constitutions, which were published in a periodical secretly subsidized by the French government, the

Affaires de l'Angleterre et de l'Amérique; he also contributed American news as well as copies of an old satire and his recent correspondence with Admiral Howe.[9] Even more important were Franklin's public appearances as the benign, rustic personification of America, complete with a fur cap he brought back from Canada. Chaumont, his landlord since the end of February, helped by commissioning sculptor Jean-Baptiste Nini to design clay medallions of Franklin for the porcelain factory Chaumont owned.[10]

Franklin's residence in a wing of Chaumont's spacious Passy home, the Hôtel de Valentinois, became the unofficial American embassy. It was full of visitors such as Frenchmen seeking commissions in the American army, captains of American merchantmen and privateers, and, all too frequently, British spies, including Edward Bancroft, an amiable friend of Deane and Franklin and a member of the British Royal Society. Franklin was largely to blame for the appalling lack of security. Warned by a fellow American of the danger of British spies, Franklin cavalierly replied that, as he had nothing to hide, he would not dismiss a valet who was a British spy, were he a good valet.[11] There is no indication, however, that Franklin had any knowledge that Bancroft was a spy or even that Bancroft and Deane were using inside information to speculate on the British stock market. So zealous a patriot that he donated his salary as postmaster general to disabled war veterans and entrusted his capital to war bonds (loan office certificates), Franklin had difficulty believing his friends less virtuous than was he.[12] Such gullibility was extremely costly, endangering American and French shipping and undermining American communication with the French government, which realized it could entrust the Americans with no confidential information about French diplomacy or military strategy. (After mid-1778 Vergennes compensated by communicating with Congress through the successive French ministers plenipotentiary in Philadelphia, Conrad-Alexandre Gérard and Anne-César, chevalier de La Luzerne.) Information provided by British spies, moreover, helped disprove French claims that it was remaining neutral.

III

In spite of British protests, most of the ships used by Beaumarchais eventually reached American ports, delivering muskets and other war supplies that proved vital to sustaining the American army.[13] Even more provocative to Britain, however, were the activities of American privateers, who operated out of French ports and sold their prizes there. The French navy needed several more months before it would be ready; while France took steps to avert a premature war, it already was soliciting the help of the large Spanish navy for the campaign of 1778.[14]

Meanwhile, Congress was no longer so unwilling to pay the price for a commercial alliance that would force France into war. As early as December 30, 1776, Congress, facing military catastrophe after the fall of New York City, decided to offer France military assistance in capturing Newfoundland and its fishery (with the United States to receive a share) and the British West Indies. Throughout 1777 it encouraged France and Spain to attack the British West Indies. In a September 25 memoir begging for more financial assistance, Franklin argued on behalf of the commissioners that depriving Britain of its monopoly of American trade would weaken the British navy while strengthening the navies of France and Spain.[15]

On November 27 the commissioners met to discuss a letter to Congress describing their current situation; the French government had promised a loan of 3 million *livres*, but insisted that French aid still be kept secret. Silas Deane argued that they should present Vergennes with an ultimatum demanding a French alliance; otherwise, America would reconcile with Britain. Franklin opposed the idea, arguing that the French would recognize the threat as hollow. His call for more patience was supported by Arthur Lee. A week later they were rewarded. Late in the morning of December 4, dispatches arrived with news that Burgoyne's entire army had been captured at Saratoga.[16]

The news of Saratoga was as opportune for Vergennes as it was for Franklin and his fellow commissioners. A memoir sent to Spain in late July had named the coming January or February as the deadline for a decision on whether to adopt a policy of direct assistance to the Americans.[17] The problem for Vergennes was the same as it had been in the spring of 1776, overcoming the scruples of Louis XVI, who did not wish war. Vergennes' strategy was similar, too. He again argued that France had no choice, because refusal to become more involved would lead to a British and American attack on the vulnerable French West Indies. Vergennes' suggestion that the Americans now would pay for British acknowledgment of their independence by joining in an attack on France was ludicrous. The commissioners did warn Vergennes that without proof of French goodwill, the American people might force Congress to take action against its wishes, but without specifying the action. Another danger was that of America making a compromise peace with Britain short of independence, but this too was implausible. Why should America, which had just won its great victory, settle for anything less than independence? In any case, the American threat was very useful in helping Vergennes overcome Louis' scruples.[18]

The British unwittingly also were of great service to Vergennes. Lord North made the mistake of sending Paul Wentworth, a secret service agent, to sound out the commissioners on American terms for peace. It also permitted Franklin's old friend the Moravian leader James Hutton and perhaps a third person, Sir Philip Gibbes, to meet with Franklin. Although Vergennes was aware of only some of the meetings, such fool's errands played into his hands, giving him ammunition to use on Louis.[19]

While awaiting the king's approval, Vergennes reconnoitered the American commissioners. At a December 5 meeting Gérard encouraged them to open negotiations, now that there were no longer any doubts about the United States' ability and resolution to maintain their independence. A few days later the commissioners responded by warning of the danger that the British would fan ill will against France among the American people, but offered reassurance that France's concluding a treaty would strengthen American resolve. Moreover, they again suggested sending French warships to American waters.

On December 12 Vergennes met with the commissioners. He disabused them of the notion that a commercial treaty alone would be adequate, as it would certainly lead to war; France needed the promise that America would not make a separate peace or give up its independence. The Americans voiced no objection, promising that France would find them "faithful and firm Allies." Vergennes warned them that formal negotiations would have to await Spain's decision on whether to join France.[20]

On December 31 Vergennes learned that Spain, with its large navy, was not willing to join the alliance with the United States. The conde de Floridablanca, the astute Spanish chief minister, believed the American commissioners were doing whatever they could to lead France and Spain into going to war for America's benefit. The following week France learned of the death of the elector of Bavaria. As the line of succession was unclear, there was a serious possibility that Austria, one of the great powers of Europe, would try to grab the entire principality, thereby upsetting the balance of power. Fortunately France, as Austria's chief ally, might be in a position to restrain them, but nevertheless there was a real danger of an unwelcome war. Vergennes' obsession with weakening Russia and Britain was so

strong that nothing could deter him from doing everything he could to help win American independence.
On January 7 he was able to persuade Louis XVI to approve formal negotiations with the commissioners.[21]

Since France and the United States had the same
goal, American independence, the negotiations were
easy. The commissioners caused no difficulty about
signing a military alliance as well as a commercial treaty; their chief worry was French reluctance to specify
when it would enter the war. (This reluctance was purely tactical; the French planned a surprise attack on the
British fleet and army at New York in the hope of ending
the war in a single blow, and they wanted to preserve
secrecy.) Moreover, Vergennes' chief purpose in using
American independence to end the British monopoly of
American trade was not economic but diplomatic. He
wished to weaken Britain's position in the balance of
power. Only as a secondary consideration did he hope
France would profit directly from American trade. (In
fact, after the war, Britain quickly recovered its domi-
nance over American trade by providing lower prices
and better service than its European rivals.) France thus
demanded no special commercial privileges to compli-
cate the negotiations. On February 6, 1778, Gérard and
the commissioners signed a treaty of alliance and a
separate treaty of amity and commerce.[22]

IV

The French government now had to balance two con-
tradictory tasks. It needed to avoid war until its fleet
had sailed for New York while preparing the French

public for the coming outbreak of hostilities. Luckily, the British government, which had immediately learned through Bancroft about the signing of the treaties, wished to delay war, too; it was sending a special peace commission to negotiate with Congress in hopes of forestalling American independence. Franklin's feelings were mixed. He hoped that Britain would recognize American independence and thus prevent the war from spreading. On the other hand, he and his colleagues, fearful that the French government might change its mind, were anxious for the treaties to be made public. In mid-March the French notified Great Britain of the signing of the commercial treaty, an insult the British could not ignore. They recalled Viscount Stormont, their ambassador at the French court, and the French soon reciprocated. There was now no reason to delay recognizing the American commissioners. On March 20 Vergennes officially introduced them to the king. Franklin promised Louis that he could rely on the gratitude of Congress and on its faithfulness to its engagements. With his spectacles and absence of a wig, Franklin, the personification of America, was an unusual sight at court.[23]

For the remainder of 1778 Franklin played a secondary role. On April 13 the French squadron for America sailed from the Mediterranean port of Toulon. Aboard the French flagship were Conrad-Alexandre Gérard, being sent to Philadelphia as the first French minister plenipotentiary, and Silas Deane, recalled by Congress for having issued numerous army commissions to unwanted Frenchmen. A few days earlier Deane's replacement, John Adams, had arrived in Paris. Diplomacy now took second place to war. Moreover, as already mentioned, Vergennes generally chose to deal directly with Congress through Gérard, rather than through the commissioners.[24] Even at the informal American mission at Passy the compulsively busy John Adams took control over routine business. Franklin did little more than sign the commissioners' letters drafted by Adams. He did, however, informally publicize the American cause, particularly by his public meetings with the great Voltaire, who was visiting Paris one last time.

The dictates of diplomatic etiquette soon changed Franklin's status. It required Congress to appoint a diplomatic representative in Paris of equal rank to Gérard. On September 14, 1778, it elected Franklin to the post and a month later approved his instructions, which were carried by the marquis de Lafayette. These included a request for French cooperation in a joint attack on Canada. Congress had not consulted with Washington, however, who lodged objections to having French troops in North America. Congress attempted to change the instructions, but Lafayette already had sailed.[25]

When the enthusiastic Lafayette reached France, he convinced Adams and Franklin that a French attack on New York, Rhode Island, or Halifax would be successful. Franklin then requested that French troops be sent to capture British-held Rhode Island, thereby clearly exceeding his instructions.[26] Fortunately for Franklin, the French were not receptive to the idea, and he was able to silently drop it without even informing

Congress of his foolish mistake. Hostilities between France and Britain began in Europe in June 1778 and in North America the following month. The French attack on New York was foiled as was a French and American attack on Newport. Moreover, with an increasing supply of sailors, the British navy was able to expand considerably. The French now had no choice but to purchase the help of the Spanish navy by offering to continue the war until the Spaniards captured Gibraltar. France also had to agree to an invasion of England, the Spaniards wishing to end the war in a single campaign, as had the French earlier. There thus were no troops available to send to America in 1779. When the invasion failed, France was receptive to shifting the focus of the war to North America. British successes in North America during the year finally changed Washington's mind about French troops. He wrote to Lafayette that he would be welcomed back to America as either an American general or the leader of a French expeditionary force. The arrival of this invitation in early 1780 persuaded the French to send troops to North America, although Lafayette was not selected to command them.[27] The more experienced comte de Rochambeau led the expeditionary force that arrived in Newport in the summer of 1780 and accompanied Washington to Yorktown the following year.

V

John Adams, who commented on Franklin's falling asleep as a congressional delegate, also criticized him for his laziness as a diplomat. His round of dinner parties, which Adams considered a sign of dissipation, has now become the norm for diplomats and legislators. Moreover, Franklin's correspondence gives evidence of how demanding and worrisome his job was and how little help he had in performing it. His clerical staff consisted of his grandson William Temple Franklin, a French secretary (first Nicolas-Maurice Gellée, then Jean L'Air de Lamotte), and in 1781 a clerk (Gurdon Mumford); he also sometimes asked friends like his landlord Chaumont and his banker Rodolphe-Ferdinand Grand for help in drafting memoranda. Although he discussed visiting his grandson Benjamin in Geneva, where the boy had been sent for his education, or visiting Italy with his other grandson, Temple, he took no vacations during his almost nine years in France. Of course, he had diversions such as music, chess, and flirtations with female neighbors like Mme Brillon and Mme Helvétius.[28] One of his greatest diversions was his printing press and type foundry, used for printing official forms and unofficial "bagatelles" (short essays and parables). He even printed longer works by authors he admired, such as the former galley slave Pierre-André Gargaz, author of a treatise on how rulers could achieve perpetual peace among their states.[29]

What did he do, in addition to helping negotiate the alliance of 1778 and the 1782–83 peace treaty with Britain? What most occupied his time and thoughts was finding money in order to support the American mission in France, to aid the American army, and to provide relief for American prisoners of war in England and escaped prisoners arriving in Passy and seeking assistance.[30] Congress, without the power to levy taxes, was no help. In several ways it made Franklin's task more onerous. It printed more and more currency without financial backing until in 1780 it had to devalue it to a fortieth of its paper value, ruining French creditors like Chaumont and humiliating Franklin. Congress continually begged him to press France for more financial aid in spite of his warnings that the French government, too, was hard pressed financially. The commissioners made the mistake of promising that France would pay the interest on American loan office certificates; as a result Franklin had to spend much of the money provided by France and huge amounts of his and Temple's time in redeeming the certificates, each of which had to be carefully checked to avoid double payment. As will be discussed in a later chapter, Congress sent a variety of other representatives to France, who in general made Franklin's life more difficult, including interfering in the vital task of wheedling more money from the French government.

Much of Franklin's time was spent on maritime matters. Captains of warships of the Continental navy were ordered to call on Franklin for assistance. Both Franklin and Chaumont were involved in outfitting the 1779 joint American-French squadron commanded by John Paul Jones. Franklin also had to certify that captures made by American privateers were of British rather than neutral ships. He also was involved in sending military supplies to America. The largest ship he used was the merchant ship *Marquis de Lafayette*, which was captured by the British while sailing to America in

1781, thereby offsetting months of work by Franklin and his grand-nephew Jonathan Williams Jr., a merchant living in Nantes.[31] Much to Franklin's relief, the able Thomas Barclay arrived in France in late 1781 to take over maritime matters, although Franklin continued to bear ultimate responsibility and a share in the work.[32]

For the four years between early 1778 and early 1782 Franklin's life was spent not in diplomatic negotiations but in the drudgery and worry of providing for the needs of Congress and his fellow Americans. His great success in this unglamorous but vital part of his mission is a testimony to his dedication, patience, and tact.

VI

Ever since Franklin's diplomatic mission, it has been very dangerous in American politics to be considered overly sympathetic to France. As one of Franklin's most astute biographers has pointed out, Franklin's need to continually urge Congress to pay attention to French feelings was motivated by pragmatic concerns, particularly America's dependence on French military and financial aid.[33] Franklin did have fond feelings for his French friends, although his circle of acquaintances generally was limited to the uppermost part of French society, particularly his neighbors in Passy and his fellow members of the Académie royale des sciences and the Neuf Soeurs masonic lodge. It is possible that he might even have spent the last years of his life in Passy had his neighbors, the Brillons, agreed to the marriage of their daughter Cunégonde to his grandson Temple.[34]

He also seems to have felt real gratitude to Louis XVI for his generosity and loyalty to the alliance. There is substantial evidence, however, that beneath this sentimental veneer, Franklin, like all good diplomats, felt real loyalty only to his own country. His attachment to France did not run very deep. He chose not to educate his younger grandson, Benjamin, in France, but instead sent him to Geneva to be raised as "a Republican and Protestant" (or, alternately, "Presbyterian").[35] Repeatedly he expressed homesickness and requested that Congress permit him to come back to America to spend his remaining years. His conduct toward the French government displayed little real gratitude. As will be discussed in the next chapter, he violated congressional instructions to consult the French government before making peace, thereby putting France in grave peril. During the peace negotiations Franklin suggested to Gérard's brother, Joseph-Mathias Gérard, now ennobled as Gérard de Rayneval, that it would be prudent once the war was over to make a new defensive alliance, thereby forgetting that the existing French-American treaty of alliance mutually guaranteed American independence and French possession of their own American colonies (i.e., the French West Indies) "from the present time and forever."[36] A decade later the French republic would learn to its disappointment that George Washington's memory was no better than Franklin's.

The most telling indictment of Franklin's coldness toward those who had made American independence possible, however, was a letter he wrote to his daughter,

Sally, in 1784. Learning of plans to found a hereditary society to honor the leading American and French military and naval veterans of the war, he mocked the idea that virtue could be inherited. He then had the letter translated into French and circulated among his friends.[37] His letter was an assault on the principles of the numerous nobly born French officers who had volunteered to serve the American cause, some of whom had died in American service. At best it was tactless, at worst a sign of arrogance. His attitude toward England, which he had once loved, was far more severe, for it was a mixture of sadness, hatred, and self-righteousness.

Chapter Five

Franklin and the British

I

ONE OF THE MANY TASKS entrusted to Franklin by
Congress during his mission to France was to help prepare a schoolbook detailing British atrocities against
Americans. In 1776 Franklin had proposed some of the
designs used on the currency issued by Congress; now
he was ordered to have 35 prints made to illustrate the
book. In May 1779 he and Lafayette compiled a detailed
list of the prints to be engraved: the burning of various
American towns, the murder of prisoners, the incite-
ment of slave rebellions, the scalping of frontiersmen
by Indians under British orders, and the plundering of
houses by British soldiers. Franklin later proposed using illustrations of British barbarities on the back of
copper coins.[1]

Franklin was an expert at political propaganda, but
the events here described generally were true and obviously made a huge impression on him. By good fortune British commanding officers like William Howe
and Henry Clinton were decent men and, like Washington, tried to mitigate the horrors of war.[2] The war,
however, did furnish many examples of the system-
atic cruelty for which the British had become notorious by their treatment of Scots, Irish, and Acadians.

Particularly heinous was the murder by neglect of more than 10,000 American sailors aboard the prison ships *Jersey* and others moored off Brooklyn. Americans were guilty of atrocities, too, although hardly on such a massive scale: a number of Loyalists, for example, were imprisoned inside the New-Gate mine in Connecticut, where some perished. As with the French Revolution, the success of the American Revolution depended not only on the enthusiasm of the faithful but on the intimidation and coercion of potential or actual adversaries.[3] Franklin was reluctant to castigate his fellow Americans for ill-treating others. Tellingly, when he learned of Christian Indians murdered by Pennsylvania frontiersmen, he wrote but deleted a reference to the Paxton Boys of 1763–64; instead, he blamed George III for inciting retribution for atrocities committed against Americans. Privately he was willing to criticize his fellow citizens for their lack of public spirit, particularly their reluctance to pay taxes, but he refrained from making adverse comments about them to Frenchmen or Britons.[4]

Franklin was not ready to turn the other cheek, although he did have reservations about imitating the British. In his April 28, 1779, instructions to John Paul Jones, he forbad him to burn defenseless British towns unless they refused to pay ransom, and he insisted that the sick, elderly, women, and children first be evacuated.[5] Franklin's attitude toward war was changing, however. In a 1780 letter to his English friend David Hartley, Franklin expressed doubts over whether there was a good war or a bad peace, a sentiment he repeated

in 1782 and 1783 letters.[6] During the 1782 peace negotiations, he sent his friend Joseph Priestley an an-
guished indictment of the savagery of warfare, express-
ing doubts about whether it was worth preserving a
species that took pride in killing and took shame in
reproducing. In the same letter he described a naval
battle as being like hell and called men worse than
devils.[7]

Franklin, as usual, could not see an evil without
attempting a remedy. In July 1782 he wrote Benjamin
Vaughan, another English friend, suggesting that farmers, fishermen, merchants on unarmed ships, and ar-
tisans should be left unmolested during wartime, an
elaboration of an idea he had expressed to friends in
1780. He enclosed a memoir comparing privateering to
piracy, since both were robbery. He eventually attempted to incorporate protection for such civilians into treaties. He was unable to persuade the British to accept
such a provision in the final peace treaty of 1783, but
just before he left France in 1785, he signed an Ameri-
can-Prussian commercial treaty that included such an
article. He enclosed a second memoir to Vaughan in July
1782, one that was part of another great humanitarian
crusade that he pursued until his death. It was a criticism of West Indian colonies because they used slaves to
produce sugar. Quoting the great philosopher Claude-
Adrien Helvétius (the late husband of his close friend
Anne-Catherine de Ligniville d'Autricourt Helvétius), he
said he regarded sugar as dyed red with their blood.[8]

Expressions of Franklin's hatred of war and slavery were far less frequent than expressions of his

hatred of George III, whom he had once idolized. He described George as thirsting for American blood. (He also accused the English nation of bloodthirstiness.) No doubt adding to his bitterness was the loss of his son William, who not only became a Loyalist but eventually, as president of the Board of Associated Loyalists, even reputedly sanctioned the murder of an American officer, Capt. William Huddy.[9] In 1783 Franklin wrote a savage satire, the "Apologue," about the Loyalists. In this parable the Americans were dogs, while the Loyalists were mongrels, a cruel comparison if Franklin had in mind his illegitimate son.[10]

This was not Franklin's first use of political satire. During the decade before the start of the Revolution, he had contributed a number of satirical political pieces to the British press.[11] Thereafter his satirical writing became infrequent. His service in Congress gave him no time for writing, so his only satire was the song lyrics mocking "The King's Own Regulars," which he probably wrote during his visit to Washington's camp at Cambridge. During his first year in France, the need for caution in not rushing the French government or appearing too radical seems to have restrained his writing. Instead, his propaganda was informal, such as mocking the British ambassador, Lord Stormont, by inspiring a new French word, *stormonter*, for "to tell a lie."[12] The first piece written in France that can be ascribed with confidence to him appeared in the *Affaires de l'Angleterre et de l'Amérique* in October 1777. Many years later, when William Temple Franklin published it in his first edition of his grandfather's papers, he called it "Comparison of Great Britain and America as to Credit, in 1777." It described America as a better credit risk than was Britain, partly because of the extravagance of George III and the corruption of the British political system, a favorite topic of Franklin's. It concluded by appealing to "generous Minds" who would take satisfaction "in opposing tyranny and aiding the Cause of Liberty which is the Cause of all Mankind."[13]

A year later, either Franklin or Arthur Lee wrote for the *Affaires* a response to the supposed British desire to soften the horrors of war, citing atrocities committed by the British against American troops in Canada.[14] Soon thereafter, the *Affaires* published a satire inspired by a manifesto of the British peace commission in America warning that Britain would use every means at its disposal to destroy or render useless the American alliance with France. It listed the bounties Britain supposedly was offering to Scots, German, and Russian mercenaries for burning towns, villages, crops, and Quaker meetinghouses, as well as for collecting scalps of women, nursing children, and others.[15] Probably it was written by Franklin, as it greatly resembles one of his most famous hoaxes, composed in 1782 just as the peace negotiations with Britain were beginning. With great care he printed two pages of a dummy issue of an actual newspaper, the *Boston Independent Chronicle*. On part of the first page he printed a fictitious letter from a Loyalist captain enclosing eight packages of scalps of American soldiers, farmers, women, boys, girls, and infants. The remainder of the first page and most of the second consisted of a fictitious letter from John

Paul Jones to Sir Joseph Yorke, British ambassador to the Netherlands, defending himself from charges of piracy and accusing the British of murdering prisoners. The remainder of the second page contained two dummy advertisements. Franklin then circulated the hoax, which was printed in both the Netherlands and England. He justified the hoax to John Adams on the grounds that, although the form might not be true, the substance was true, as more people had been scalped than were enumerated in the invoice.[16] Franklin thus entered the peace negotiations full of rage at the British government and at the Loyalists. He tried to keep that rage hidden, but he had limited success.

II

On November 19, 1781, Elkanah Watson, a 23-year-old American merchant transplanted to France, dined with Franklin at Passy. According to Watson's diary, Franklin entertained his young visitor by playing on the glass armonica, a musical instrument of his own invention. Joined by Edward Bancroft, they then discussed the news from America. Admiral de Grasse had entered Chesapeake Bay, the combined armies of General Washington and General Rochambeau were marching toward Virginia, and a French squadron had sailed from Newport to join de Grasse. If all went well, General Cornwallis would be trapped at Yorktown. They wondered, however, what would happen if the British fleet en route from New York intercepted the Newport squadron. They brought out maps. Franklin alternated between despondency and exhilaration.

At 11 p.m. Watson departed for his hotel, fearing the British would escape. Right after his departure, a messenger arrived with the news that Cornwallis had surrendered with his entire army.[17]

The victory at Yorktown was a rare example of selfless cooperation among allies, including the Spaniards, who gave great assistance to de Grasse's fleet.[18] Franklin's skill in negotiating loan after loan had helped keep Congress from total bankruptcy and the American army from disintegration until the victory at Yorktown had been achieved.

It was not clear, however, exactly to what the victory would lead. Lord North realized that his strategy of regaining America on the battlefield was now hopeless. He had no intention, however, of giving up the effort to achieve by guile what could not be achieved by force, attempting without success to divide Britain's enemies by making a separate peace with France, the Netherlands, or the United States. He even sent an American, Thomas Digges, to The Hague to meet with Adams, the American minister designate to the Netherlands. Digges also suggested coming to Passy, but unsurprisingly received no encouragement to do so; he had embezzled money meant for American prisoners, and Franklin's hatred of him was unbounded.[19] Meanwhile, although an informal truce existed in North America, the war continued elsewhere, particularly in the Caribbean.

Although the English public blamed the North government for mismanaging the war, it took several months for the opposition to North in the House of Commons to come together. On February 27, 1782, the opposition finally won a vote stating that those advocating an offensive policy against the Americans were enemies to their country. Three weeks later North resigned office rather than face a vote of no confidence.[20]

The policy of the next government was not completely different from North's, however. Most of its members and supporters wished to make peace with America so as to be able to better make war on Britain's other enemies, France, Spain, and the Netherlands. This was a policy that posed great dangers to the United States. It was still dependent on France for financial assistance. If it made a peace agreement with Britain only to see Britain force France to leave the war, the United States would be helpless should Britain repudiate its agreement and resume the fight. It required all of Franklin's guile to negotiate a safe ending to the war. Moreover, he was not empowered to conduct the negotiations alone. Congress originally had intended John Adams to negotiate both the peace treaty and a commercial treaty with Britain, but Vergennes, distrustful of Adams's loyalty, ability, and perhaps even sanity, successfully lobbied Congress in 1781 to have his commissions revoked. Congress then entrusted the negotiations to a commission of five members: Franklin, Adams, Minister to Spain John Jay, Minister to the Netherlands Henry Laurens (who had been captured by the British and imprisoned in the Tower of London), and Thomas Jefferson. To further please France, Congress, by now reduced to virtual beggary, ordered the commissioners not to make peace without the "Knowledge and Concurrence" of France.[21]

III

The new British government was a diverse coalition headed by the ineffectual Marquess of Rockingham. Hitherto, the foreign office had been divided between a secretary of state for northern Europe and another for southern Europe. George III ended this unwieldy arrangement by naming the popular Charles James Fox as secretary of state for foreign affairs, but this established an even more problematical division of responsibility. William Petty, Earl of Shelburne, a former secretary of state, was named secretary of state for home and colonial affairs. He and Fox were bitter rivals, and each wanted control of the American negotiations. Shelburne had several advantages. As secretary of state for the southern department fifteen years earlier, he had been responsible for colonial affairs and had been on very good terms with Franklin.[22] What is more, he now could claim that unless American independence was recognized, the Americans were still subjects of the king and hence were part of his responsibilities. Perhaps most important, Franklin presented Shelburne with an opportunity to move first. An English nobleman who had made the acquaintance of Mme Brillon called on Franklin and volunteered to carry a letter to Shelburne. Franklin immediately wrote to congratulate Shelburne on the recent actions of the House of Commons and to convey the thanks of Mme Helvétius for the gooseberry bushes that Shelburne, an old friend, had sent her. Immediately upon receiving Franklin's letter, Shelburne sent Richard Oswald, an elderly friend of Laurens, to meet with Franklin; he arrived on April 14, 1782. Fox in turn sent a young member of Parliament, Thomas Grenville, to meet with Vergennes and possibly Franklin, but he did not reach Paris until May 7.[23]

The competition between Shelburne and Fox was more than personal, as the two men had vastly different aims. Unlike most of his colleagues, Shelburne was anxious to make peace with France, but he also hoped to preserve some sort of connection between Britain and the United States, whereas Fox was willing to concede American independence if the United States would abandon France to British attack. Franklin thus was given a chance to play off Shelburne against Fox as well as France against Britain. In Shelburne, however, he confronted a shrewd negotiator.[24]

At their first meeting at Passy (on April 15), Oswald told Franklin that the English public expected the Americans to make a separate peace. Franklin replied that they must act in communication with the French, but he was cordial to his visitor. He predicted that once peace was made, Britain and America would be good friends and that Britain would regain a large share of its commerce with America. Two days later he took Oswald to court and introduced him to Vergennes. This cordiality was deceptive, however. Franklin was still full of rage over British war atrocities. At a later meeting just before Oswald returned to London for instructions, Franklin responded to Oswald's proposal that he at least make some suggestions about British-American terms. He suggested that if the British wished not only peace but reconciliation, they should give Canada to the United States in reparation for the atrocities committed by the British army and its Indian allies. A few days later Franklin sent Adams a copy of his savage newspaper hoax.[25]

As a result of Oswald's visit, Franklin invited his fellow peace commissioners to join him. To Franklin's disappointment, Jefferson declined appointment as a peace commissioner (as he had turned down an appointment as commissioner in 1776) and remained in America. Laurens eventually declined to participate in the negotiations because of his health, and Adams, who had replaced Laurens in the Netherlands, was unwilling to leave for Paris until he had completed negotiations for a Dutch-American commercial treaty. Jay accepted, but he did not arrive in Paris until June 23 and soon was stricken with influenza, leaving Franklin to negotiate on his own.[26]

IV

The British cabinet soon approved conducting parallel negotiations in Paris, with Oswald negotiating with Franklin while Grenville negotiated with Vergennes; it proposed granting independence to the United States if Spain and France returned everything they had captured from Britain (including Minorca, West Florida, and several valuable West Indian islands). Secretly Oswald was ordered to sound out Franklin about a federal union between Britain and the United States; Shelburne rejected the idea of surrendering Canada. Oswald resumed discussions with Franklin on May 4.

Three days later Grenville arrived and soon was taken by Franklin to meet Vergennes. The French minister rejected the terms proposed by the cabinet, as he claimed that the Americans did not need to ask for independence. He said that they had declared it without receiving any encouragement from France; Franklin, who knew better, kept silent.[27]

For much of May Oswald was back in London for further instructions, leaving Grenville to conduct discussions with Franklin. Even the British cabinet was indecisive about who was to negotiate with Franklin; it recommended that Fox instruct Grenville to offer a royal acknowledgment of American independence prior to the start of formal negotiations, but it also recommended sending Oswald back to Paris. On June 1 Grenville made his offer. Franklin apparently had encouraged both Oswald and Grenville to believe that America was willing to make peace without France; to Grenville's astonishment, Franklin rejected his offer. Two days later he told Oswald that he preferred to negotiate with him. He claimed that he chose Oswald over Grenville because he liked him and believed him more knowledgeable about America.[28] Whether inadvertently or not, Franklin made a shrewd choice. Accepting Grenville's offer would have been extremely risky on several grounds. Nothing was said about issues such as boundaries, so accepting the offer of a recognition of independence would have left the Americans little leverage in subsequent negotiations. Moreover it would have undermined French trust in Franklin's sincerity. Finally it would have been unwise to place confidence in Fox, who, unlike Shelburne, was distrusted by George III. Oswald may have furthered his cause by hinting, untruthfully, that, unlike Fox, Shelburne might not be opposed to surrendering Canada.

Franklin's good judgment (or good luck) soon was confirmed. On July 1 Rockingham died. Shelburne succeeded him as prime minister and assumed direct control over all the peace negotiations, while Fox was dismissed from office. Upon learning the news Franklin took the initiative by presenting Shelburne with his conditions for making peace. He delivered to Oswald on July 10 a list of four necessary conditions: (1) full and complete American independence and withdrawal of all British troops; (2) a boundary settlement; (3) Canada to be confined to its boundaries before the 1774 Quebec Act, thereby giving the United States the region west of the Appalachians; and (4) Americans to receive fishing and whaling rights on the Newfoundland Banks and elsewhere. He also listed four advisable articles: (1) indemnification of Americans whose towns had been burned; (2) a public apology for the harm done to America; (3) Americans ships and trade to have the same privileges in Britain and Ireland as did British ships and trade; and (4) Britain to give up every part of Canada. His advisable articles, although unlikely to be accepted, apparently were a sincere attempt to produce a reconciliation that he hoped would, as Franklin told a British friend, in a few years heal wounds and lead to great prosperity. Franklin now broke off discussions with Oswald and prepared to wait until Shelburne gave in. It took barely two weeks. On July 27 Shelburne

informed Oswald he would be sent full powers to con-
clude a treaty on the basis of the necessary articles.[29]

Shelburne needed an agreement with the Americans to pressure France and Spain into making peace,
having as yet made no progress in negotiations. Moreover, he believed that the United States quickly would
become economically dependent on Great Britain, a
far more realistic assessment than Vergennes' expec-
tation that American trade would be divided among
various trading partners. In his letter to Oswald, Shelburne expressed the hope that a treaty could be concluded quickly. Unfortunately John Jay, now restored
to health, objected to the wording of Oswald's draft
commission, which did not acknowledge the United
States as independent. Franklin felt the commission
was acceptable but, hating disputes with his colleagues, agreed to a delay. Within days Franklin was
bedridden with an attack of kidney or bladder stones
so severe that apparently he feared his life was in danger. For a month the negotiations were in the hands of
John Jay. They resumed only when the British issued a
revised commission (a meaningless concession because
it could be repudiated if negotiations failed).[30]

The lost weeks were important. By the time the
new commission arrived on September 27, the British
negotiating position had been greatly strengthened
by Britain's repulse of a Spanish attack on Gibraltar.
The British no longer felt the same pressure to make
concessions on the American-Canadian border, and the
American commissioners eventually settled for what is
today's boundary instead of one that would have given

the United States what is today southern Ontario.[31] As Franklin and Jay awaited the arrival of Adams from the Netherlands, Franklin persuaded a reluctant Jay to agree to the appointment of William Temple Franklin as secretary to the peace commission, much to the later annoyance of Adams, who had his own candidate in mind.[32] After Adams's arrival in Paris on October 26, negotiations were conducted intensively for five weeks. To Adams's surprise, Franklin made no objection to the peace commissioners' disregarding the instructions of Congress to keep France informed of their progress, even though Franklin said that he believed the French court's intentions were honorable. Franklin's cooperation with his colleagues is not surprising, as Oswald testified that Franklin's loyalties were exclusively to the United States. Adams praised Franklin for his sagacity and said that the three commissioners worked "in entire Harmony and Unanimity." This, too, is unsurprising. As a native Bostonian, Franklin was as avid for fishing rights as was Adams, and no one in America was keener on American expansion than was Franklin; he had written Jay in 1780 that selling a drop of the Mississippi River would be like selling his street door to a neighbor. Doubtless, too, Franklin was glad to have two lawyers as able as Jay and Adams to make sure that every i was dotted and every t crossed. On one issue Franklin was more uncompromising than his colleagues (as Adams later admitted). Shelburne was anxious to obtain some compensation for the Loyalists, fearing their opposition to the peace treaty; Franklin was adamantly against it and even raised the issue of

Britain's compensating Americans for their losses to counter the proposal. In the end Britain had to settle for an article that Congress would recommend to the states that the Loyalists' property be restored, an article that eventually proved meaningless.[33]

The preliminary American-British peace agreement, which was signed on November 30, 1782, was conditional upon Britain and France signing a treaty. Stretching a point, it could be said to fulfill the terms of the Franco-American treaty that neither party sign a separate treaty. It also could be said to comply with the commissioners' instructions from Congress to consult with France before signing a treaty. In practice, the agreement was of great benefit to the British and put France in grave danger; had French negotiations with Britain miscarried, Congress would have had difficulty getting its war-weary constituents to continue fighting. Without American pressure on the remaining British garrisons in the United States, Britain could have withdrawn forces from North America to attack the French West Indies.

Knowing there would be great opposition in Parliament to the terms of the treaty, which gave generous borders and fishing rights to the United States, Shelburne avoided another political dispute by withdrawing a tentative peace agreement already reached with France and Spain by which Spain would have obtained Gibraltar. (France was obligated by its treaty with Spain not to make peace until Spain obtained Gibraltar.) Vergennes was outraged by the American agreement, which he blamed on Franklin's colleagues. To add to the insult, Franklin reminded Vergennes of his request for another loan for the United States. When Vergennes sent a protest, Franklin's response was cleverly phrased but menacing. He apologized for the peace commissioners' "Indiscretion" and said he hoped the English would find themselves mistaken in believing they had divided France and the United States. Still dependent on the support of the Continental Army, Vergennes was not in a position to continue the argument, which, by good fortune, had lost some of its sting. Pedro Pablo Abarca de Bolea, conde de Aranda, the Spanish ambassador at the French court, had agreed during the interval between the two letters to surrender the Spanish demand for Gibraltar, accepting instead West and East Florida and Minorca. On January 20 Spain and France signed their own agreements with Britain, and the American agreement with Britain came into force.[34]

V

The preliminary peace agreement left unsettled important matters like commercial relations between the United States and Britain. The commissioners expected these to be resolved in the final peace treaty, which would be negotiated after the end of hostilities. In December 1782 both Adams and Franklin privately composed lists of items they hoped would be included in it. Among Franklin's were an end to privateering, the protection of farmers and merchants in case of war, joint citizenship for residents of Britain and the United States with free entry of their ships into each other's ports, and the independence of Canada, Nova

Scotia, and Bermuda with a right for them to join the United States.[35] Alleyne Fitzherbert, a professional diplomat who took over from Oswald in mid-January, was outraged, however, at the "monstrous injustice" of amending the preliminary treaty; he considered Franklin an inveterate enemy of Britain who was animated by "private animosity and resentment" and who would do his utmost to prevent the revival of good relations, if he was given a chance.[36] Thus, for the first few months after the January 20, 1783, general armistice, the British made no move to reopen discussions. Franklin hoped to pressure Britain by withholding the opening of American ports to British ships, much to the annoyance of Fitzherbert. But Americans, desperate for British goods, welcomed ships of all nations, including Britain, to their ports.[37] Nevertheless, Franklin was busy during this period. At the request of Sweden, Congress had appointed him to negotiate a commercial treaty between their nations. He and the Swedish ambassador to the French court handled the negotiations successfully, although John Adams was upset that he and Jay had been excluded from the discussions; the treaty even included a limited prohibition of privateering.[38] He also commissioned two elegant objects commemorating American independence: the "Libertas Americana" medal that he helped design, and a book of French translations of the American state constitutions, treaties, and other public documents. Both were distributed to members of the diplomatic corps as well as prominent Frenchmen and other Europeans; copies of the medal also were sent to members of Congress.[39]

Finally, discussions for a final treaty began in May. The commissioners were encouraged by the choice of Franklin's good friend David Hartley, a former member of the House of Commons, as negotiator, but the discussions were hopeless. Fox was once again British foreign secretary, and he repeatedly beat down all of Hartley's attempts to give a liberal interpretation to his instructions. The key point desired by the Americans was access for American ships to the British West Indies. In early July George III prohibited it, a clear indication that the discussions in Paris were hopeless. Franklin tried to win acceptance of an additional treaty article protecting civilians from the effects of war, but it, too, was rejected. At the beginning of September, the commissioners and Hartley signed a final treaty merely confirming the terms reached the previous November and formalized in January. The British government continued to treat the United States with contempt, refusing to evacuate its posts in the interior of America because the United States, in violation of the treaty, discriminated against former Loyalists.[40]

Soon thereafter Franklin's health deteriorated, and he gradually became less capable of leaving Passy. He did negotiate a consular treaty with France, but it was rejected by Congress because it was thought to infringe on American sovereignty; Franklin's successor, Thomas Jefferson, later negotiated a new treaty. Homesick and ill, Franklin repeatedly asked permission to return to America. Congress, however, had a new job for him. In the spring of 1784, it appointed a new commission to negotiate commercial treaties with more than twenty

European and African countries. It sent Jefferson to join Franklin and Adams. (Jay and Laurens had returned to America.) The members of the commission cooperated amicably, with Jefferson taking the lead in preparing treaties, but few countries responded. The one success they enjoyed before Franklin was finally permitted to depart in the summer of 1785 was a commercial treaty with Prussia. This treaty did include Franklin's beloved article protecting civilians in the extremely unlikely case of a future war between Prussia and the United States.[41]

During Franklin's return voyage to America, his ship stopped briefly in England where he entertained visitors. Most were friends from his years spent in England. One, however, was his son William. Benjamin treated him coldly and forced him to sign over his property in New Jersey to William Temple Franklin.[42] He never forgave William for becoming a Loyalist. Once again we encounter the Benjamin Franklin of the war years. Given our usual image of the kindly, tolerant Franklin, it is jarring to see him as an angry, embittered, hard-core revolutionary, but this, too, is part of who he was. Beneath his self-control was a man of strong passions. His hatred of the British Crown, on which Fitzherbert remarked, doubtless was based in part on bitterness at the loss of his beloved son, but it had wider causes, as the visits of his friends must have reminded him. He had fought to save America's connection with Britain and to avoid war, but his trust had been betrayed. The Britain he had so loved was now lost to him as irrevocably as was his youth.

Although Franklin's diplomatic career ended in 1785, he did not forget the way American weakness had led to British abuse. One of his last public acts, as we shall see, was his participation in the drafting of a new constitution to make America better equipped to protect itself. Franklin's long mission to France taught him not only about foreigners but also about his fellow Americans. Not all the lessons were pleasant.

Chapter Six

Franklin and His Fellow Americans

I

DURING HIS EIGHTEEN MONTHS in Congress, Franklin was one of the most radical delegates. He was among the quickest to grasp the hopelessness of petitioning the British government and hence the necessity of revolution. His opponents in Congress were the laggards and, worse still, those like his old friend Joseph Galloway who were unable to make the final break with the old order of things. By leaving Congress a few months after the Declaration of Independence, he was spared most of the subsequent factional infighting within that body. He did have to endure, however, many disputes with his fellow Americans on diplomatic missions in Europe. Not only were these disputes uncomfortable for someone like Franklin who hated contestation; they also put him in a position to which he had become unaccustomed. Now he was accused of being insufficiently zealous and even of being subservient to foreigners. The accusations against Franklin were no less painful for being false; he was, for tactical reasons, a diplomatic traditionalist, but he was no conservative, particularly in his relations with the British government, which no one hated more strongly.

Part of Franklin's difficulties came from his tendency to believe the best of those for whom he cared. He eventually learned a particularly bitter lesson about excessive trust as a result of his friendship with his fellow commissioner Silas Deane, who became embroiled in a lengthy dispute with Congress about his accounts and then in 1781 wrote a number of defeatist letters that the British intercepted and published. Once Franklin learned of Deane's abandonment of the American cause, he broke decisively with him. Franklin also came under suspicion of using his position for personal profit. There is no evidence, however, that Franklin engaged in profiteering nor that he knew about Deane and Bancroft's speculations on the London stock market.[1]

Even more dangerous than Deane and Bancroft was a rash young Marylander named William Carmichael, who in the summer of 1777 also abused Franklin's trust. The notorious privateer captain Gustavus Conyngham outraged the French government by sending prizes into French ports. In response to French complaints, the commissioners sent Carmichael to deliver orders to Conyngham to return to America without taking any more prizes. Instead, Carmichael, perhaps in conjunction with Deane, encouraged him to cruise against British shipping, apparently in the hope of forcing the French government to end its neutrality. The resulting crisis briefly threatened a premature and surely disastrous war with Britain that France averted by expelling from St. Malo a squadron of American warships. Carmichael's folly resulted in the capture of one American ship and the loss at sea of another, Wickes's *Reprisal*, which had brought Franklin to France.[2]

Most of the problems in the American mission, however, came not from betrayed trust but from clashing egos. Two disputes were particularly damaging because Franklin thereby became the enemy of his colleagues Arthur Lee and Ralph Izard, who returned to America in 1780 and became influential congressional delegates. These men were intelligent and patriotic, but exasperating. Lee was so suspicious that Franklin drafted (but did not send) a letter to him warning that he was liable to become insane. Izard, who, in the words of John Adams, had irritable nerves and very strong passions, was so self-important that Franklin wrote a satire of him, "The Petition of the Letter Z." Franklin, however, later blamed himself for causing Izard's enmity by not complimenting him. Franklin also had a policy dispute with Izard. After Lee's unsuccessful missions to Spain and Prussia in 1777, Franklin developed a strong antipathy to uninvited diplomatic missions or "militia diplomacy," feeling that the United States should act like a "virgin state" and wait to be courted; Izard was minister designate to the Grand Duke of Tuscany, and he resented being excluded from discussions with the commissioners to France.[3]

Franklin's most important relationships in France were with his fellow peace commissioners, John Adams, John Jay, and Henry Laurens. Franklin's relationship with Adams had been generally harmonious during their eighteen months in Congress, and this continued during most of the time they spent as fellow commissioners in France from early 1778 to early 1779. Adams objected to Franklin's round of parties, while he, ever the good Puritan, passed his spare time studying French and international politics. He tried to be a peacemaker between Franklin and Lee and to organize the commission's disorderly papers. His relationship with Franklin abruptly changed when he was left without a job after the commission was abolished and Franklin was named minister plenipotentiary. When Adams lost the chance to return to America on an American warship and instead was given passage on a smaller French frigate, he became convinced that Franklin wanted him captured by the British.[4]

Adams returned to Europe in late 1779 in order to participate in future peace talks and commercial treaty negotiations with Britain. He alarmed Vergennes by wishing to notify the British government of his mission. He then vociferously defended Congress for devaluating American currency to a fortieth of its former value, ruining many French investors such as Chaumont. Franklin attempted to mollify Vergennes by criticizing Adams; he also criticized Adams to Congress. When Vergennes ceased communicating with Adams, the latter left France for the Netherlands. (Henry Laurens, the American minister designate to the Netherlands, soon was captured at sea by the British, and Adams undertook his duties.) When Congress revoked Adams's powers to negotiate peace with Britain, he blamed Franklin. Adams was so angry that when he came to Paris in October 1782 for the peace negotiations he had to be talked into calling on Franklin.

Relations improved during the peace negotiations, with Adams praising Franklin's conduct, but deteriorated thereafter. Already upset that he had not been consulted in the naming of a secretary for the commission, Adams was disturbed by Franklin's negotiating with Sweden without consulting the other commissioners. (Franklin also upset him by drafting passports for British ships without consulting his colleagues.) Finally Franklin wrote American foreign secretary Robert Livingston that Adams, although meaning well, was sometimes "absolutely out of his senses," an insult that got back to Adams. Although Adams was too confrontational, suspicious, and self-righteous to be an effective diplomat, Franklin was not blameless for the dispute between them. It was important not to jeopardize relations with France, but questioning Adams's sanity in letters to America was unnecessarily provocative. Although Franklin had a passion for his own reputation and fame (as Adams commented in his diary), his motive for criticizing Adams seems to have been professional rather than personal; Franklin's overriding concern in France was preservation of the French alliance on which America depended.[5]

Franklin's relationship with John Jay was the opposite of his relationship with Adams. He told Jay that he would like him to be his successor if Congress accepted his resignation. When Jay and his family arrived in France in 1782, he treated Jay's charming wife and daughter as if they were part of his own family. Unfortunately, his trust in Jay was misplaced. During the period of Franklin's illness in the midst of the peace discussions, Jay badly mishandled the negotiations with Britain. As already noted, he needlessly delayed formal negotiations, giving the British time to improve their military position and hence their bargaining position. He also crudely let Shelburne know his willingness to abandon the French alliance and to make a separate peace, whereas Franklin left his position ambiguous in order to protect the alliance. Perhaps worst of all, Jay encouraged the British to recapture West Florida from Spain. Jay was embittered by his treatment at the Spanish court and by his negotiations in Paris with the Spanish ambassador, the conde de Aranda, and believed Britain more likely than Spain to share navigation of the Mississippi River. Thus he was willing to betray France's close ally Spain, an ally that had made an indispensable contribution to American independence by forcing the British to keep much of their navy in European waters to protect England and Gibraltar. Fortunately the British did not take up Jay's suggestion, although the preliminary peace agreement promised more generous borders for West Florida if the British recaptured it (an article kept secret from France that was rightfully criticized by Congress). Jay's morally reprehensible proposal could have had a devastating effect on American history had the British regained West Florida and kept East Florida at the peace. It is hard to see how the United States could subsequently have obtained Florida from Britain. Ultimately, a British Florida would have made the abolition of slavery far more difficult, because it would have been impossible to blockade the southern states if they rebelled. In spite of Jay's misconduct, he remained on good terms with Franklin, and when he returned to the United States in 1784 he was elected as American secretary of state for foreign affairs. As such he had little direct dealings with Franklin, but he did write a severe critique of the consular treaty with France that Franklin had negotiated.[6]

Franklin's relationship with Henry Laurens also was cordial. Laurens, in ill health after his long captivity in the Tower of London, spent part of his time in England trying to regain his health and part of the time in France, where his brother and daughters were living; he reached Paris in time to participate during the final day of the peace negotiations.[7] Franklin sympathized with his problems and showed great kindness and consideration to him.

Unfortunately Franklin's relationship with Laurens's son John, one of George Washington's staff officers, was less good. Impatient at not receiving more loans from France, Congress sent the young man to France in 1781 to obtain supplies for Washington's army. Franklin, who obtained another loan before Laurens's arrival, was very upset at Congress's lack of trust and offered his resignation. (Fortunately Congress did not accept it.) John Laurens performed an enormous service to the American cause before he even left Lorient, the port where his ship arrived. Learning that the marquis de Castries, the French naval minister, was expected to pass through the city, he decided to wait for him. At their meeting he informed Castries of the desperate condition of the American army, information which Castries doubtless passed on to Admiral De Grasse, whom Castries met at Brest just before De Grasse's departure for the Caribbean. The admiral's splendid cooperation with Washington may have been partly the result of Laurens's encounter with Castries.

John Laurens's subsequent mission had mixed success. He did procure more financial aid, but he alienated the French by purchasing war supplies in the Netherlands rather than France. He then created an enormous amount of work for Franklin when two ships hired by his secretary, Maj. William Jackson, to carry the goods failed to sail from Amsterdam with their escorting frigate. Relations between Laurens and Franklin were proper but rather strained, and Franklin doubtless was glad to see him return to America.[8]

Franklin's most difficult colleagues were lesser agents of Congress like Thomas Morris, Robert Morris's alcoholic half-brother, and William Lee, Arthur's brother, who briefly served as co-agents in Nantes of the Secret Committee; Lee later created a diplomatic crisis by signing without authorization a commercial agreement with an unofficial agent from the Netherlands. Franklin, fearing accusations of nepotism, prevented his grand-nephew Jonathan Williams Jr. from obtaining a similar commercial post—without informing him! Williams performed various services for the commissioners, such as supervising the repair of muskets for the Continental army, but, unknown to Franklin, even he was not immune to profiteering. He smuggled luxury goods aboard ships going to America. He also fought a duel with Arthur Lee's nephew.[9]

Franklin's opinion of his American diplomatic colleagues tended to be extremely critical or overly trusting, depending on whether or not he considered them his friends. Elkanah Watson wrote in his journal that Franklin loved adulation.[10] An excess of self-regard is a common failing for revolutionaries, but Franklin's displeasure led to no more than harsh words in his correspondence. The leaders of the French Revolution were not so mild-mannered.

II

Franklin's relations with Congress also were affected by misunderstandings and by an occasional lack of tact on both sides. Franklin was frustrated by Congress's continual demands for more money from France, its lack of sensitivity to French feelings, and its failure to provide him with an embassy secretary and a consul to help with his heavy workload. Congress in turn was disturbed by Franklin's difficulties in obtaining more and larger loans from the French government. It also was frustrated by the shortage of news from him, particularly compared with the frequent and lengthy letters from John Adams and John Jay. This difficulty in communication was caused in part by a shortage of ships and reliable couriers to carry Franklin's letters across a wide ocean patrolled by many British ships (like the one which captured Henry Laurens). By his own admission, however, Franklin had become adverse to writing letters; even those persons he loved, such as his daughter, Sally, and his sister, Jane, did not often hear from him. (His friend Mme Helvétius teased him that he loved people only when he was with them.)[11] In his defense, the letters he did write were informative and perceptive, and he had his own complaints about the lack of news and instructions from Congress.

In spite of its complaints, Congress elected him four times as its representative abroad (as commissioner to France, minister plenipotentiary to France, peace commissioner, and member of the commission to make commercial treaties). It ignored, however, his requests for a post for his grandson William Temple Franklin, probably in part because of suspicion that he might be influenced by his Loyalist father, William.[12] Congress did not recall Franklin in 1779 as it did other American ministers like Izard and Lee.[13] In large part Franklin's survival was due to his friendship with leaders of the various factions in Congress, from the conservative finance minister, Robert Morris, to the radical secretary of the Committee for Foreign Affairs, Thomas Paine.[14] The friendship with Morris, the most important American politician during the second half of the Revolution, was particularly important. Both Franklin and Morris understood that eighteenth-century warfare was as much a contest of economies as it was of cultures.[15] Because of runaway inflation, America came extremely close to an economic collapse that would have destroyed its independence, much as inflation later destroyed the economy and undermined the independence of the Confederate States of America. Franklin, who had extensive experience in both war and business, well understood what was involved. Like

Morris, he vainly urged American self-reliance, based on individual and collective frugality and independence. He and Morris realized how the war effort was undermined by the states failing to provide Congress with the money it needed. For lack of an alternative, Congress resorted to printing money without backing until its currency collapsed in 1780. Thereafter it was totally dependent on French financial support, as was demonstrated by the instructions it gave the peace commissioners. Franklin realized this, too, and supported Vergennes in his dispute with Adams about the devaluation of American currency. Franklin and Morris were partners in keeping the United States from complete economic collapse.[16] The French, for reasons of self-interest, were willing to keep Congress solvent; Franklin's subtle combination of tact and threat facilitated this assistance rather than hindering it, unlike the crude tactics of Adams.

Ultimately, Franklin survived politically because of his usefulness. One of his strongest defenders was a young man he had yet to meet, the nationalist delegate from Virginia, James Madison.[17] The most severe criticism of his diplomacy was the rebuke he and his fellow peace commissioners received for disregarding their instructions to consult France before making a peace treaty, but this criticism was accompanied by praise for the favorable peace terms they had obtained.[18] His diplomatic approach based on realism and accommodation with France was controversial, but finally it was successful. Ironically, he was punished by Congress not for failure but for success. Wanting desperately to return home after the conclusion of the final peace treaty, he was denied permission for another year and a half because Congress felt he was still needed in France. This left him with little to do until he finally returned to America in the summer of 1785.

Epilogue

Franklin Returns to Philadelphia

FRANKLIN RETURNED TO an America different from the one he had left nine years earlier but in some ways similar. After enormous difficulties, America had won its independence, but many prewar problems remained—class differences, disputes between the states, and economic dependence on a Britain that dominated American trade and still despised Americans, as shown by its refusal to evacuate Detroit and other frontier posts.[1] Without an independent income, Congress was unable to enforce unity on the states. Without economic independence, American political independence was incomplete.

Franklin's revolutionary zeal had been based on a vision of an orderly, prosperous, expanding America. Once freed from the control of narrow-minded, selfish British officials and politicians, an independent America would be able to grow. Because new obstacles had arisen to prevent American independence and growth, Franklin needed a new approach. He did not blame America's problems on social injustice or economic inequality, as this would have required him to jettison a lifetime's view of America as a promised land. Instead he viewed America's problems as temporary ones caused by political instability. To restore order,

Franklin returned to the politics of his youth, a politics based on reasoned discussion and compromise.

Franklin's main arena was Pennsylvania, the state with the most highly developed political parties and the most confrontational politics. The Constitutionalists favored retention of the radical 1776 state constitution, including its unicameral legislature. The opposing Republicans favored giving the wealthy more political power by adopting a bicameral legislature. When Franklin returned to Pennsylvania, he was elected president of the Pennsylvania Supreme Executive Council (roughly equivalent to being a governor with very limited power). He had the support of both political parties, each of which expected his support. His own program was to accommodate both parties and thereby ease the political tension. He was successful enough to be elected to two more yearlong terms, the most allowed by the Pennsylvania Constitution, although in the process he undermined the Constitutionalist Party by expanding the electorate to include more of its political enemies.[2] In 1786 his friend Benjamin Rush praised his success in destroying party rage, comparing it to Franklin's famous scientific experiment of calming the waters by pouring oil on them.[3] His success, however, was ephemeral. Pennsylvania would see bitter social and political conflict through the 1790s, and his grandson Benjamin Franklin Bache would be a major participant in it.

While still in office, Franklin was selected to attend the Constitutional Convention of 1787. As an ardent nationalist acutely aware of America's vulnerability to foreign domination, he advocated strengthening the central government. Like the other delegates, he was a supporter of order and property rights and an opponent of radical democracy, as was shown by his opposition to Shays's Rebellion in Massachusetts; he signed a March 10, 1787, proclamation of the Supreme Executive Council offering a reward for the capture of Daniel Shays.[4] He had not lost all of his democratic ideals, however, as was demonstrated by the positions he took at the convention. He was suspicious of executive power. He fought against giving presidents an absolute veto over legislation, and he was in favor of impeachment for malpractice or dereliction of duty. He even tried to deny presidents a salary or stipend. He paid tribute to the American people's public spirit, citing in particular the patriotism of the American prisoners of war he had assisted. He favored making it easy to become a citizen and difficult to be convicted of treason. He successfully opposed limiting suffrage to men of property. He failed, however, to win support for a unicameral legislature like Pennsylvania's. Instead, the convention agreed to a compromise supported by Franklin in which the states were given equal representation in the Senate and unequal representation in the House of Representation. Franklin's main concern was preventing a breakdown of discussion, the culmination of a lifetime of working as a conciliator and consensus builder. His work at the convention and his support for the new constitution were invaluable to its success.[5]

Once his work at the convention and as president of the Supreme Executive Council was complete, Franklin finally retired at age 82 in hopes of finishing his autobiography. He embraced, however, a final cause he could support with his pen, that of abolishing slavery.[6]

Franklin was not an automatic supporter of the common man; after his experiences with the Paxton Boys, he had a strong dislike of mobs (and frontiersmen). In many ways he resembles the Thermidorians who ruled France between the fall of Robespierre and the rise of Napoleon; they, too, supported revolution but hated mobs, were uncomfortable with violence, supported territorial expansion, and thought Britain corrupt. Franklin was, however, in some ways more radical than they were. He never lost his hatred of injustice, that indispensable part of any revolutionary's soul. Nor, for that matter, did he ever lose his self-righteousness, his supreme self-confidence, his capacity for anger, his pragmatism, and his political skill, which, too, are the traits of a successful revolutionary.[7] Franklin's role in the American Revolution was the logical extension and culmination of his political career.

Notes

1. From Rebelliousness to Prosperity

1. See, for example, Edmund S. Morgan, *Benjamin Franklin* (New Haven: Yale University Press, 2002), 29–30. Various biographies of Franklin are discussed in "Recommended Reading."

2. His autobiography describes his life between his birth in 1706 and his 1757 departure for England on behalf of the Pennsylvania Assembly. See Leonard W. Labaree et al., eds., *The Autobiography of Benjamin Franklin*, 2nd ed. (New Haven: Yale University Press, 2003). The best secondary accounts of Franklin's early life are the first volume of J. A. Leo Lemay, *The Life of Benjamin Franklin*, 3 vols. (Philadelphia: University of Pennsylvania Press, 2006–9) and Arthur Bernon Tourtellot, *Benjamin Franklin: The Shaping of Genius, the Boston Years* (Garden City NY: Doubleday, 1977).

3. For his hatred of disputes and his claims to having no enemies as a man, see his unsent April 3, 1778, letter to Arthur Lee in Leonard W. Labaree et al., eds., *The Papers of Benjamin Franklin*, 39 vols. to date (New Haven: Yale University Press, 1959–), 26:223, and his January 6, 1784, letter to John Jay in Albert Henry Smyth, ed., *The Writings of Benjamin Franklin*, 10 vols. (New York: Macmillan, 1905–7), 9:151.

4. For example, Franklin to Jonathan Shipley, Feb. 24, 1786, in Leo Lemay, ed., *Benjamin Franklin: Writings* (New York: Library of America, 1986), 1161–63. With it Franklin may have enclosed his essay "The Internal State of America": Verner W. Crane, "Franklin's 'The Internal State of America' (1786)," *William and Mary Quarterly*, 3rd series, 15 (1958): 214–27. See also Smyth, *Writings of Franklin*, 9:472–73, 492–94; 10:52.

5. Robert Middlekauff, *Benjamin Franklin and His Enemies* (Berkeley: University of California Press, 1996) is a brilliant treatment of the subject.

6. See James Tagg, *Benjamin Franklin Bache and the* Philadelphia Aurora (Philadelphia: University of Pennsylvania Press, 1991).

7. A good introduction is Henry F. May, *The Enlightenment in America* (New York: Oxford University Press, 1976).

8. David Waldstreicher, *Runaway America: Benjamin Franklin, Slavery, and the American Revolution* (New York: Hill and Wang, 2004) is a stimulating account.

9. For Franklin's value system, two older books are still very useful: Paul W. Conner, *Poor Richard's Politicks* (New York: Oxford University Press, 1965) and Gerald Stourzh, *Benjamin Franklin and American Foreign Policy*, 2nd ed. (Chicago: University of Chicago Press, 1976). Worthy recent companions to these are Lorraine Smith Pangle, *The Political Philosophy of Benjamin Franklin* (Baltimore: Johns Hopkins University Press, 2007) and Alan Houston, *Benjamin Franklin and the Politics of Improvement* (New Haven: Yale University Press, 2008).

10. In 1789 he opposed amending the Pennsylvania constitution to create an upper house elected by the wealthy: Smyth, *Writings of Franklin*, 10:58–60.

11. For his reaction to the Paxton Boys, see chapter 2, below; for his reaction to Shays's Rebellion, see the epilogue. His dislike of London mobs is discussed in Jack P. Greene, "The Alienation of Benjamin Franklin, British American," in Greene, *Understanding the American Revolution: Issues and Actors* (Charlottesville: University Press of Virginia, 1995), 272–73.

12. For his views on poverty, see his May 9, 1753, letter to Peter Collinson in Labaree, *Papers of Benjamin Franklin*, 4:480. For his views on private property, see his December 25, 1783, letter to Robert Morris in Lemay, *Franklin: Writings*, 1079–83.

13. Labaree, *Papers of Benjamin Franklin*, 37:170.

14. Lemay, *Life of Benjamin Franklin*, 2:25.

15. Pauline Maier, *The Old Revolutionaries: Political Lives in the Age of Samuel Adams* (New York: Alfred A. Knopf, 1980), 8–9.

16. Lemay, *Life of Benjamin Franklin*, 1:3–52; Lemay, *Franklin: Writings*, 5–42; Labaree, *Papers of Benjamin Franklin*, 1:8–45.

17. Lemay, *Life of Benjamin Franklin*, 3:176–216; Lemay, *Franklin: Writings*, 323–44; Houston, *Benjamin Franklin and the Politics of Improvement*, 106–46.

18. Waldstreicher, *Runaway America*, 23.

19. See Lemay, *Life of Benjamin Franklin*, 1:215–317. For patronage and deference in prerevolutionary America, see Gordon S. Wood, *The Radicalism of the American Revolution* (New York: Alfred A. Knopf, 1992), 3–92.

20. Labaree, *Papers of Benjamin Franklin*, 4:225–34.

21. Gary B. Nash, *The Unknown American Revolution: The Unruly Birth of Democracy and the Struggle to Create America* (New York: Viking Penguin, 2005), 1–206. Richard Hofstadter, *America at 1750: A Social Portrait* (New York: Alfred A. Knopf, 1971) downplays social conflict at midcentury.

22. Lemay, *Franklin: Writings*, 975–83.

23. Lemay, *Franklin: Writings*, 359–61; Lemay, *Life of Benjamin Franklin*, 3:224–30; Labaree, *Papers of Benjamin Franklin*, 4:130–33.

24. The best account of Franklin's family life is still Claude-Anne Lopez and Eugenia Herbert, *The Private Franklin* (New York: Norton, 1975). For Deborah's importance to the family business, see Lemay, *Life of Benjamin Franklin*, 2:3–37.

25. Lemay, *Life of Benjamin Franklin*, 1:332–56; 2:356–75, 402–19; 3:176–216, 265–86.

26. Labaree, *Papers of Benjamin Franklin*, 3:180–212, 308–16; Lemay, *Life of Benjamin Franklin*, 3:1–57; Houston, *Benjamin Franklin and the Politics of Improvement*, 60–105; William S. Hanna, *Benjamin Franklin and Pennsylvania Politics* (Stanford CA: Stanford University Press, 1964), 32–34.

27. Lemay, *Life of Benjamin Franklin*, 3:497–514; J. Bennett Nolan, *General Benjamin Franklin: The Military Career of a Philosopher* (Philadelphia: University of Pennsylvania Press; London: Humphrey Milford, Oxford University Press, 1936); Leonard W. Labaree, "Benjamin Franklin and the Defense of Pennsylvania, 1754–1757," *Pennsylvania History* 29 (1962): 7–23.

28. Labaree, *Papers of Benjamin Franklin*, 22:224-41, 274-77.

29. Lemay, *Life of Benjamin Franklin*, 2:322-57, 462-66.

2. Two Missions to England

1. Hanna, *Benjamin Franklin and Pennsylvania Politics*, 72-73; Lemay, *Life of Benjamin Franklin*, 3:336-39; Marc Egnal, *A Mighty Empire: The Origins of the American Revolution* (Ithaca NY: Cornell University Press, 1988), 76-79.

2. Fred Anderson, *Crucible of War: The Seven Years' War and the Fate of Empire in British North America* (New York: Alfred A. Knopf, 2000), 5-7, 46-65. For the background to the crisis, see Jonathan R. Dull, *The French Navy and the Seven Years' War* (Lincoln: University of Nebraska Press, 2005), 12-18.

3. Labaree, *Papers of Benjamin Franklin*, 5:344-53, 357-92, 397-417; Lemay, *Life of Benjamin Franklin*, 3:375-91, 613-23; Houston, *Benjamin Franklin and the Politics of Improvement*, 148-75; Robert C. Newbold, *The Albany Congress and Plan of Union of 1754* (New York: Vantage, 1955); Timothy J. Shannon, *Indians and Colonists at the Crossroads of Empire: The Albany Conference of 1754* (Ithaca NY: Cornell University Press, 2000).

4. Francis Jennings, *Benjamin Franklin, Politician* (New York: W. W. Norton, 1996), 49-56.

5. For Franklin's role in arranging logistical support for Braddock, see Labaree, *Papers of Benjamin Franklin*, 6:13-22, 25-26, 59; Lemay, *Life of Benjamin Franklin*, 3:423-35; Whitfield J. Bell and Leonard W. Labaree, "Franklin and the 'Wagon Affair,' 1755," *Proceedings of the American Philosophical Society* 101 (1957): 551-58; and Alan Houston, "Benjamin Franklin and the 'Wagon Affair' of 1755," *William and Mary Quarterly*, 3rd series, 66 (2009): 235-86.

6. Dull, *French Navy and the Seven Years' War*, 26-34, discusses the outbreak of hostilities.

7. Hanna, *Benjamin Franklin and Pennsylvania Politics*, 77-116; James H. Hutson, *Pennsylvania Politics, 1746-1770: The Movement for Royal Government and Its Consequences* (Princeton: Princeton University Press, 1972), 6-40.

8. Good introductions are I. Bernard Cohen, *Benjamin Franklin's Science* (Cambridge: Harvard University Press, 1990) and Philip Dray, *Stealing God's Thunder: Benjamin Franklin's Lightning Rod and the Invention of America* (New York: Random House, 2005). For a summary of his electrical discoveries, see Lemay, *Life of Benjamin Franklin*, 3:58-137.

9. For the number of troops, see Dull, *French Navy and the Seven Years' War*, 107-9, 145. The best study of Pitt's role in the British victory is Richard Middleton, *The Bells of Victory: The Pitt-Newcastle Ministry and the Conduct of the Seven Years' War, 1757-1762* (New York: Cambridge University Press, 1985). For changes in British colonial administration, see James A. Henretta, *"Salutary Neglect": Colonial Administration under the Duke of Newcastle* (Princeton: Princeton University Press, 1972), 283-347, and Jack R. Greene, "The Origins of the New Colonial Policy, 1748-1763," in Jack P. Greene and J. R. Pole, eds., *A Companion to the American Revolution* (Malden MA: Blackwell, 2000), 101-11. For Franklin's growing disillusionment with the English people and the British political system, see Jack R. Greene, "Alienation of Benjamin Franklin" and "Pride, Prejudice, and Jealousy: Benjamin Franklin's Explanation for the American Revolution," both in Greene, *Understanding the American Revolution*, 48-71, 247-84.

10. Hanna, *Benjamin Franklin and Pennsylvania Politics*, 126-27; Hutson, *Pennsylvania Politics*, 44-45.

11. For Franklin's unsuccessful mission, see Hanna, *Benjamin Franklin and Pennsylvania Politics*, 117-39; Hudson, *Pennsylvania Politics*, 41-72; Middlekauff, *Benjamin Franklin's Enemies*, 55-76.

12. Sheila Skemp, *William Franklin: Son of a Patriot, Servant of a King* (New York: Oxford University Press, 1990) is an excellent biography of Franklin's son. See also Lemay, *Life of Benjamin Franklin*, 2:3-9, and Lopez and Herbert, *The Private Franklin*, 22-23, 59-69, 92-94.

13. Franklin's pamphlet is in Labaree, *Papers of Benjamin Franklin*, 9:47-100. The peace negotiations are discussed in Dull, *French Navy and the Seven Years' War*, 191-206, 228-44.

14. Gregory Dowd, *War under Heaven: Pontiac, the Indian Nations, and the British Empire* (Baltimore: Johns Hopkins University Press, 2002); Colin G. Calloway, *The Scratch of a Pen: 1763 and the Transformation of North America* (Oxford: Oxford University Press, 2006); Richard Middleton, *Pontiac's War: Its Causes, Course, and Consequences* (New York: Routledge, 2007).

15. Lemay, *Franklin: Writings*, 540–58; Hanna, *Benjamin Franklin and Pennsylvania Politics*, 148–53; Labaree, *Papers of Benjamin Franklin*, 11:22–30, 42–75, 80–86.

16. Waldstreicher, *Runaway America*, 194–95.

17. See John Murrin, "The French and Indian War, the American Revolution, and the Counterfactual Hypothesis: Reflections on Lawrence Henry Gipson and John Shy," *Reviews in American History* 1 (1973): 307–18, and Jack P. Greene, "The Seven Years' War and the American Revolution: The Causal Relationship Reconsidered," *Journal of Imperial and Commonwealth History* 8 (1979–80): 85–105.

18. Lemay, *Franklin: Writings*, 374. One of the "Palatine Boors," although I have found no evidence of him in Franklin's shop book (Labaree, *Papers of Benjamin Franklin*, 2:127–28), was my great-great-great-great-great-grandfather, John Peter Dull (originally Doll or Döll), who arrived in Philadelphia from the Palatinate in 1737.

19. Hutson, *Pennsylvania Politics*, 84–177, discusses the connection between the Paxton Boys and the 1764 election. See also Hanna, *Benjamin Franklin and Pennsylvania Politics*, 154–68; Labaree, *Papers of Benjamin Franklin*, 11:390–95.

20. Hutson, *Pennsylvania Politics*, 181–90.

21. John Brewer, *The Sinews of Power: War, Money, and the English State, 1688–1783* (New York: Cambridge University Press, 1976), 30, 39–40; John Shy, *Toward Lexington: The Role of the British Army in the Coming of the American Revolution* (Princeton: Princeton University Press, 1965), 45–139.

22. Labaree, *Papers of Benjamin Franklin*, 12:47–61, 145–46n, 234–35; 21:125–28.

23. A brilliant recent book contrasts the failure of British policy in North America with its success in India, where local elites were enlisted in support of British policy: P. J. Marshall, *The Making and*

Unmaking of Empires: Britain, India, and America, c. 1750–1783 (Oxford: Oxford University Press, 2005). Most American authors have not recognized the legitimacy of some of the British grievances against the colonists; Franklin certainly did not. For American smuggling with the French during the Seven Years' War and the resentment it engendered, see Thomas M. Truxes, *Defying Empire: Trading with the Enemy in Colonial New York* (New Haven: Yale University Press, 2008).

24. The standard history is Edmund S. Morgan and Helen M. Morgan, *The Stamp Act Crisis: Prologue to Revolution* (Chapel Hill: University of North Carolina Press, 1953). See Labaree, *Papers of Benjamin Franklin*, 12:271–74, for Deborah Franklin's account of the defense of Franklin's house and 13:124–62 for his testimony to the House of Commons.

25. For the colonial agents, see Michael G. Kammen, *A Rope of Sand: The Colonial Agents, British Politics, and the American Revolution* (Ithaca NY: Cornell University Press, 1968).

26. Greene, "Alienation of Benjamin Franklin," in Greene, *Understanding the American Revolution*, 273–79; Middlekauff, *Franklin and His Enemies*, 123–25; Labaree, *Papers of Benjamin Franklin*, 17:160–65. In a 1773 letter, Franklin admitted the constraints on the king: Labaree, *Papers of Benjamin Franklin*, 20:277–86. The idea that the king and Parliament were indissolubly linked was virtually universal among Britons: William B. Willcox, "Franklin's Last Years in England: The Making of a Rebel," in Melvin H. Buxbaum, ed., *Critical Essays on Benjamin Franklin* (Boston: G. K. Hall, 1987), 104.

27. Labaree, *Papers of Benjamin Franklin*, 19:399–413; 20:268–86, 380–81, 513–16, 539–80; 21:5–9, 13–23, 31–34, 37–75, 85–96, 99–101, 197–202, 414–35.

28. Jonathan R. Dull, *A Diplomatic History of the American Revolution* (New Haven: Yale University Press, 1985), 38; Michael Roberts, "Great Britain and the Swedish Revolution, 1772–73," *Historical Journal* 7 (1964): 1–46. For a survey of the ensuing crisis, see David Ammerman, "The Tea Crisis and Its Consequences, through 1775," in Greene and Pole, *Companion to the American Revolution*, 195–205. The most detailed account is Benjamin Woods Labaree, *The Boston Tea Party* (New York: Oxford University Press, 1964).

29. Labaree, *Papers of Benjamin Franklin*, 21:130–34, 152–53, 155–57.

30. Labaree, *Papers of Benjamin Franklin*, 21:212–16, 222–22, 235–36.

31. Labaree, *Papers of Benjamin Franklin*, 21:540–99. Other documents concerning the negotiations are Labaree, *Papers of Benjamin Franklin*, 21:360–68, 376–86, 405–11, 436–37, 444–45, 456–68, 479–82, 491–503, 514–15, 526–29, 531–34.

32. Labaree, *Papers of Benjamin Franklin*, 21:398–99, 472–79, 569–70, 579–83.

33. Labaree, *Papers of Benjamin Franklin*, 21:498, 572–73, 584–85, 589–90. Franklin made a similar statement in 1755: Lemay, *Life of Benjamin Franklin*, 3:480.

34. Labaree, *Papers of Benjamin Franklin*, 21:400–404, 593.

35. Labaree, *Papers of Benjamin Franklin*, 21:13–18, 197–202, 526n, 526–28, 534–35.

3. Eighteen Months in Congress

1. Hanna, *Benjamin Franklin and Pennsylvania Politics*, 196–97; H. James Henderson, *Party Politics in the Continental Congress* (New York: McGraw-Hill, 1974), 72–73, 86–87; Jack N. Rakove, *The Beginnings of National Politics: An Interpretive History of the Continental Congress* (New York: Alfred A. Knopf, 1979), 100.

2. For Galloway's relationship with Franklin, see Benjamin H. Newcomb, *Franklin and Galloway: A Political Partnership* (New Haven: Yale University Press, 1962).

3. Labaree, *Papers of Benjamin Franklin*, 22:32–34. For William Temple Franklin's date of birth, see Labaree, *Papers of Benjamin Franklin*, 22:67n.

4. Labaree, *Papers of Benjamin Franklin*, 22:xlix–xl, 33n, 35–36, 72–74, 126–28, 131–34, 512–15.

5. Labaree, *Papers of Benjamin Franklin*, 21:275–76n; 22:50–51, 57–60. As Franklin knew, most Moravians were not fully pacifists: Lemay, *Life of Benjamin Franklin*, 3:505.

6. Labaree, *Papers of Benjamin Franklin*, 22:72, 85, 92, 199–201.

7. Labaree, *Papers of Benjamin Franklin*, 22:98–99, 280–81.

8. Labaree, *Papers of Benjamin Franklin*, 22:112–25.

9. Labaree, *Papers of Benjamin Franklin*, 22: xli–xlii, 159–61, 172–73, 175–77, 179–82, 186–87, 342–44; 25:78, 101–2; North Callahan, *Henry Knox: General Washington's General* (New York: Rinehart, 1958), 33–60; James L. Nelson, *George Washington's Secret Navy: How the American Revolution Went to Sea* (New York: McGraw-Hill, 2008), 78–79.

10. Labaree, *Papers of Benjamin Franklin*, 22:163–67; Nelson, *Washington's Secret Navy*. The best account of the work of the Secret Committee is Elizabeth M. Nuxoll, *Congress and the Munitions Merchants: The Secret Committee of Trade during the American Revolution, 1775–1777* (New York: Garland, 1985).

11. Daniel A. Baugh, "The Politics of British Naval Failure, 1775–1777," *American Neptune* 52 (1991): 221–46; Richard Buel Jr., *In Irons: Britain's Naval Supremacy and the American Revolutionary Economy* (New Haven: Yale University Press, 1998). For the naval side of the war, see Jonathan R. Dull, *The French Navy and American Independence: A Study of Arms and Diplomacy, 1774–1787* (Princeton: Princeton University Press, 1975), and *The Age of the Ship of the Line: The British and French Navies, 1650–1815* (Lincoln: University of Nebraska Press, 2009), 91–117.

12. Labaree, *Papers of Benjamin Franklin*, 22:217, 223–41, 246–47, 274–77. For Washington's army, see Charles Royster, *A Revolutionary People at War: The Continental Army and American Character, 1775–1783* (Chapel Hill: University of North Carolina Press, 1979).

13. Labaree, *Papers of Benjamin Franklin* , 22:251–52.

14. Labaree, *Papers of Benjamin Franklin*, 22:280–81, 287–91, 296–97. For Dumas, see Jan Willem Schulte Nordholt, *The Dutch Republic and American Independence*, trans. Herbert H. Rowen (Chapel Hill: University of North Carolina Press, 1982).

15. For Vergennes' early political career, see Orville T. Murphy, *Charles Gravier, Comte de Vergennes: French Diplomacy in the Age of Revolution, 1719–1787* (Albany: State University of New York Press, 1982), 3–207.

16. Labaree, *Papers of Benjamin Franklin*, 22:310–18, 453–54;

Dull, *French Navy and the Seven Years' War*, 7, 44, 73, 157–58, 168, 249–54; Dull, *French Navy and American Independence*, 30–31.

17. Labaree, *Papers of Benjamin Franklin*, 22:354–56, 369–74. Franklin also provided Deane with a letter of introduction to Dumas: Labaree, *Papers of Benjamin Franklin*, 22:374–75.

18. A good brief account of the Canadian invasion is James L. Nelson, *Benedict Arnold's Navy: The Ragtag Fleet That Lost the Battle of Lake Champlain but Won the American Revolution* (Camden ME: International Marine/McGraw-Hill, 2006), 72–219, but see also Justin H. Smith, *Our Struggle for the Fourteenth Colony: Canada and the American Revolution*, 2 vols. (New York: C. P. Putnam's Sons, 1907), 1:304–604; 2:1–458; James Kirby Martin, *Benedict Arnold, Revolutionary Hero: An American Warrior Reconsidered* (New York: New York University Press, 1997), 104–222; Hal T. Shelton, *General Richard Montgomery and the American Revolution* (New York: New York University Press, 1994), 79–150; Michael P. Gabriel, *Major General Richard Montgomery: The Making of an American Hero* (Madison NJ: Fairleigh Dickinson University Press; London: Associated University Press, 2002), 82–172. I have made some of the same criticisms about Napoleon's invasion of Egypt: Dull, *Age of the Ship of the Line*, 150–51.

19. Labaree, *Papers of Benjamin Franklin*, 22:lii, 350–53, 379–86, 397–401, 413–32, 438–42; Smith, *Our Struggle for the Fourteenth Colony*, 2:317–24, 343; Nelson, *Benedict Arnold's Navy*, 182–99. For Franklin's role in Carroll's advancement, see Jules A. Baisneé, *France and the Establishment of the American Catholic Hierarchy: The Myth of French Interference (1783–1784)* (Baltimore: Johns Hopkins University Press, 1934).

20. Labaree, *Papers of Benjamin Franklin*, 21:325–26, 515–18; 22:li–lii, 356–58, 367–68, 388–89, 392–94, 400–402, 485–86; Julian P. Boyd, *The Declaration of Independence: The Evolution of the Text as Shown in Facsimiles of Various Drafts by Its Author, Thomas Jefferson* (Princeton: Princeton University Press, 1945), 16–28; L. H. Butterfield et al., eds., *Diary and Autobiography of John Adams*, 4 vols. (Cambridge: Belknap Press of Harvard University Press, 1961), 3:335–37. There are a number of biographies of Paine, but perhaps the best introduction

would be his writings themselves: Eric Foner, ed., *The Complete Writings of Thomas Paine*, 2 vols. (New York: Citadel Press, 1945). For a provocative article on the relationship between foreign affairs and the Declaration, see James H. Hutson, "The Partition Treaty and the Declaration of American Independence," *Journal of American History* 58 (1971–72): 877–96; for overviews, see Pauline Maier, *American Scripture: Making the Declaration of Independence* (New York: Alfred A. Knopf, 1997), and David Armitage, *The Declaration of Independence: A Global History* (Cambridge: Harvard University Press, 2007).

21. Labaree, *Papers of Benjamin Franklin*, 22:512–15; Jackson Turner Main, *The Sovereign States, 1775–1783* (New York: New Viewpoints, 1973), 133–34, 153–56, 218–20; Douglas M. Arnold, *A Republican Revolution: Ideology and Politics in Pennsylvania, 1776–1790* (New York: Garland, 1989), 40–57.

22. Labaree, *Papers of Benjamin Franklin*, 22:453–54, 487–90; Dull, *French Navy and American Independence*, 30–53, 340–41; Dull, *French Navy and the Seven Years' War*, 253. For Beaumarchais' role in the war, see Brian N. Morton and Donald Spinelli, *Beaumarchais and the American Revolution* (Latham MD: Lexington Books, 2003).

23. Labaree, *Papers of Benjamin Franklin*, 22:483–84, 518–21, 591–94, 596–605; Ira D. Gruber, *The Howe Brothers and the American Revolution* (New York: W. W. Norton, 1972), 117–20; Butterfield, *Diary and Autobiography of John Adams*, 3:337–38.

24. Labaree, *Papers of Benjamin Franklin*, 22:453–71, 473–74, 501–2, 624–25.

25. Labaree, *Papers of Benjamin Franklin*, 22:624–30; Robert J. Taylor et al., eds., *Papers of John Adams*, 15 vols. to date (Cambridge: Belknap Press of Harvard University Press, 1977–), 4:260–302; Foner, *Writings of Paine*, 1:16–19; Felix Gilbert, *To the Farewell Address: Ideas of Early American Foreign Policy* (Princeton: Princeton University Press), 3–75; James H. Hutson, "Intellectual Foundations of Early American Diplomacy," *Diplomatic History* 1 (1977): 1–19.

26. There is a good biography of Wickes by the able naval historian William Bell Clark: *Lambert Wickes, Sea Raider and Diplomat: The Story of a Naval Captain of the Revolution* (New Haven: Yale University Press, 1932).

27. Labaree, *Papers of Benjamin Franklin*, 22:551–53; Skemp, *William Franklin*, 192–226.

28. Labaree, *Papers of Benjamin Franklin*, 23:23–28.

4. FRANKLIN AND THE FRENCH

1. There is a delightful collection of documents written by the members of the diplomatic corps and descriptions of various members of it: Jules Flammermont, *Rapport à M. le ministre de l'instruction publique sur les correspondances des agents diplomatiques étrangers en France avant la révolution, conservées dans les archives de Berlin, Dresde, Genève, Turin, Gênes, Florence, Naples, Simancas, Lisbonne, Londres, La Haye et Vienne* (Paris: Imprimerie nationale, 1896).

For discussion of Franklin by various Italian diplomats, see Antonio Pace, *Benjamin Franklin and Italy* (Philadelphia: American Philosophical Society, 1958). I have discussed Franklin's diplomatic career in a previous book and article that contain considerable information not in the present book: *Franklin the Diplomat: The French Mission* (Philadelphia: American Philosophical Society, 1982, published as *Transactions* 72, part 1) and "Benjamin Franklin and the Nature of American Diplomacy," *International History Review* 5 (1983): 346–63.

2. For Dana's mission, see Labaree, *Papers of Benjamin Franklin*, 34:188–89, 514–15, 517–19. Most of the pre–French Revolution diplomatic instructions have been published by the Commission des Archives Diplomatiques as *Recueil des instructions données aux ambassadeurs et ministres de France depuis les traités de Westphalie jusqu'à la révolution française*, 30 vols. to date (Paris: Félix Alcan, 1884–).

3. Mary A. Giunta et al., eds., *The Emerging Nation: A Documentary History of the Foreign Relations of the United States under the Articles of Confederation, 1780–1789*, 3 vols. (Washington DC: National Historical Publications and Records Commission, 1996), 1:892; Dull, *Franklin the Diplomat*, 65. For Starhemberg's skill, see Dull, *French Navy and the Seven Years' War*, 89–94.

4. For Franklin's election as vénérable, see Labaree, *Papers of Benjamin Franklin*, 29:528–30. An introduction to his social life and

reputation is provided by Alfred Owen Aldridge, *Franklin and His French Contemporaries* (New York: New York University Press, 1957). See also Stacy Schiff, *A Great Improvisation: Franklin, France, and the Birth of America* (New York: Henry Holt, 2005).

5. For the latter, see Henry L. Roberts, "Maxim Litvinov," in Gordon A. Craig and Felix Gilbert, eds., *The Diplomats, 1919-39* (Princeton: Princeton University Press, 1953), 344-77.

6. Labaree, *Papers of Benjamin Franklin*, 23:85n. For Chaumont, see Thomas J. Schaeper, *France and America in the Revolutionary Era: The Life of Jacques-Donatien Leray de Chaumont, 1725-1803* (Providence RI: Berghahn Books, 1995).

7. Labaree, *Papers of Benjamin Franklin*, 37:liv-lv, 169-72, 295-97.

8. Labaree, *Papers of Benjamin Franklin*, 23:82, 89-90, 113-14, 117-24, 126-27, 132-40, 164-66, 173-82, 194-99, 329-39, 383-84, 493-95, 501-3, 514-17; 24:517; Dull, *French Navy and American Independence*, 49-56, 60-69, 352-53. For the Farmers General, see Jacob M. Price, *France and the Chesapeake: A History of the French Tobacco Monopoly, 1674-1791, and Its Relationship to the British and American Tobacco Trade*, 2 vols. (Ann Arbor: University of Michigan Press, 1973).

9. Labaree, *Papers of Benjamin Franklin*, 23:213-14, 288, 375-76, 430, 477-78, 481n, 521, 606-7; 24:53-54, 167-68, 229-30, 272-73, 508-14; 25:93-94, 168, 310, 327, 540-41, 627; 26:52, 154-57, 211, 623-27; 27:155n, 623-27; 28:256-59. His first original piece for the *Affaires* was written in October 1777; see the following chapter. For the commissioners' other activities during 1777, see Dull, *Franklin the Diplomat*, 19-26.

10. Labaree, *Papers of Benjamin Franklin*, 23:155, 244-46; Schaeper, *Chaumont*, 25-26, 128-29.

11. Labaree, *Papers of Benjamin Franklin*, 23:162-63; 211-12. My good friend Thomas Schaeper was kind enough to send me a copy of his forthcoming biography, *Edward Bancroft: Scientist, Author, Spy* (New Haven: Yale University Press, 2010), which promises to be the definitive study of the British spy effort. Schaeper has made good use, among other sources, of the numerous documents reproduced

in Benjamin Franklin Stevens, compiler, *Facsimiles of Manuscripts in European Archives Relating to America, 1773–1783*, 25 vols. (London: privately printed, 1889–98). Prior works on this subject are to be used with extreme caution, particularly Julian P. Boyd, "Silas Deane: Death by a Kindly Teacher of Treason?" *William and Mary Quarterly*, 3rd series, 16 (1959): 165–87, 319–42, 515–50.

12. Labaree, *Papers of Benjamin Franklin*, 22:218–19; 23:280–81n.

13. Morton and Spinelli, *Beaumarchais and the American Revolution*, 73–115, 125–43.

14. Dull, *French Navy and American Independence*, 83–87.

15. Labaree, *Papers of Benjamin Franklin*, 23:96–100; 24:13–14, 102, 553–63.

16. Labaree, *Papers of Benjamin Franklin*, 25:134–35, 207–8, 234–37, 245.

17. Dull, *French Navy and American Independence*, 86, 91.

18. Labaree, *Papers of Benjamin Franklin*, 25:260–61, 282–85; Dull, *French Navy and American Independence*, 94–97; C. H. Van Tyne, "Influences Which Determined the French Government to Make the Treaty with America, 1778," *American Historical Review* 21 (1915–16): 532–33; Chris Tudda, "'A Messiah That Will Never Come': A New Look at Saratoga, Independence, and Revolutionary War Diplomacy," *Diplomatic History* 32 (2008): 779–810.

19. Labaree, *Papers of Benjamin Franklin*, 25:305–7, 401–4, 412, 419–24, 435–40; Dull, *French Navy and American Independence*, 89–97.

20. Labaree, *Papers of Benjamin Franklin*, 25:246, 260–61, 282–85, 305–9.

21. Labaree, *Papers of Benjamin Franklin*, 25:440; Dull, *French Navy and American Independence*, 93–99; John Hardman and Munro Price, eds., *Louis XVI and the Comte de Vergennes: Correspondence, 1774–1787* (Oxford: Voltaire Foundation, 1998), 3–154.

22. Labaree, *Papers of Benjamin Franklin*, 25:440–52, 521–23, 548–49, 583–629, 684; Dull, *French Navy and American Independence*, 99–101, 341.

23. Labaree, *Papers of Benjamin Franklin*, 25:270n, 562–63,

581-82, 712-14; 26:18, 39-40, 47-48, 120, 138-41, 159, 173-74, 188-90, 195-96; Dull, *Franklin the Diplomat*, 43-44.

24. See John Joseph Meng, ed., *Conrad Alexandre Gérard: Despatches and Instructions* (Baltimore: Johns Hopkins University Press, 1935).

25. Labaree, *Papers of Benjamin Franklin*, 27:407-9, 633-46, 654-55.

26. Labaree, *Papers of Benjamin Franklin*, 28:603-6.

27. Dull, *French Navy and American Independence*, 112-62, 190; Dull, *Diplomatic History of the American Revolution*, 114-18.

28. The most reliable guide to Franklin's flirtations is Claude-Anne Lopez, *Mon Cher Papa: Franklin and the Ladies of Paris* (New Haven: Yale University Press, 1966). For Adams's comments about Franklin, see Butterfield, *Diary and Autobiography of John Adams*, 2:346; 4:118-19; Dull, *Franklin the Diplomat*, 65.

29. Labaree, *Papers of Benjamin Franklin*, 29:lxiii-lxiv, 347n, 726-27, 750-57; 30:345-47; 32:174n; 33:102-5; 34:xxxii, 321-25; 35:lxi; 37:lviii, 607-8, 611-14; 38:lxiv; Ellen R. Cohn, "The Printer at Passy " in Page Talbott, ed., *Benjamin Franklin: In Search of a Better World* (New Haven: Yale University Press, 2005), 235-71.

30. For Franklin's work on behalf of prisoners, see Catherine M. Prelinger, "Benjamin Franklin and the American Prisoners of War in England during the American Revolution," *William and Mary Quarterly*, 3rd series, 32 (1975): 261-94; Sheldon S. Cohen, *Yankee Sailors in British Gaols: Prisoners of War at Forton and Mill, 1777-1783* (Newark: University of Delaware Press; London: Associated Universities Press, 1995) and *British Supporters of the American Revolution, 1775-1783: The Role of 'Middling-Level' Activists* (Woodbridge, Eng.: Boydell Press, 2004), 22-82.

31. Claude-Anne Lopez, "Benjamin Franklin, Lafayette, and the *Lafayette*," *Proceedings of the American Philosophical Society* 108 (1964): 181-223. For the military supplies for Congress, see Labaree, *Papers of Benjamin Franklin*, 31:267-69; 32:269; 33:166-67; 34:473-75.

32. For Barclay, see Priscilla H. and Richard S. Roberts, *Thomas Barclay (1728-1793): Consul in France, Diplomat in Barbary* (Bethlehem PA: Lehigh University Press, 2008).

33. Stourzh, *Benjamin Franklin and American Foreign Policy*, 147–85. For French loans and grants see Labaree, *Papers of Benjamin Franklin*, 37:633–40; 38:487–88; 39:201–6; Dull, *Franklin the Diplomat*, 49–50. I have discussed the range of Franklin's activities in *Franklin the Diplomat*, 45–46.

34. Labaree, *Papers of Benjamin Franklin*, 31:324; 34:lix–lx, 560–63.

35. Labaree, *Papers of Benjamin Franklin*, 29:351, 357–58, 614; 34:140.

36. Labaree, *Papers of Benjamin Franklin*, 25:590; 37:335

37. Smyth, *Writings of Franklin*, 9:161–68.

5. Franklin and the British

1. Labaree, *Papers of Benjamin Franklin*, 22:xxv, 357–58; 29:522, 590–93; 30:430; 31:439; 38:lix n.

2. For Howe, see Gruber, *Howe Brothers*; for Clinton, see William B. Willcox, *Portrait of a General: Sir Henry Clinton in the War of Independence* (New York: Alfred A. Knopf, 1964).

3. Ray Raphael, *A People's History of the American Revolution: How Common People Shaped the Fight for Independence* (New York: New Press, 2001) provides a useful corrective to the popular sanitized version of the American Revolution. Reciprocal atrocities were particularly common in South Carolina, but occurred in other places; for example, see Raphael, *People's History*, 169, for the hanging of Loyalists in Morristown, New York, who refused to join the American army. See also Edward Countryman, *A People in Revolution: The American Revolution and Political Society in New York, 1760–1790* (Baltimore: Johns Hopkins University Press, 1981), 169–75.

4. Labaree, *Papers of Benjamin Franklin*, 37:586–88, 666–67; 38:488–89.

5. Labaree, *Papers of Benjamin Franklin*, 29:386–87.

6. Labaree, *Papers of Benjamin Franklin*, 31:437; 37:457; Smyth, *Writings of Franklin*, 9:93–96.

7. Labaree, *Papers of Benjamin Franklin*, 37:444–45.

8. Labaree, *Papers of Benjamin Franklin*, 32:466–67, 476;

37:608-11, 617-20; 38:433-35, 444-45, 584-85; 39:569-70; Giunta, *Emerging Nation*, 1:872, 910; 2:809-10. For Franklin's gradual conversion to abolitionism, see Houston, *Benjamin Franklin and the Politics of Improvement*, 200-216, and Waldstreicher, *Runaway America*.

9. Labaree, *Papers of Benjamin Franklin*, 25:653-54; 28:462; 32:119-20n; 36:102; 38:294n; Skemp, *William Franklin*, 257-65.

10. Labaree, *Papers of Benjamin Franklin*, 39:232-34. Franklin's persona in the parable was a noble horse, one of the rare occasions Franklin praised an animal not uniquely American, such as rattlesnakes or wild turkeys.

11. Franklin's prewar satirical writings are collected in Verner W. Crane, ed., *Benjamin Franklin's Letters to the Press, 1758-1775* (Chapel Hill: University of North Carolina Press, 1950). The relevant volumes of Labaree, *Papers of Benjamin Franklin* reprint these writings.

12. Stevens, *Facsimiles of Manuscripts*, 18: no. 1648.

13. Labaree, *Papers of Benjamin Franklin*, 24:508-14; 25:169n.

14. Labaree, *Papers of Benjamin Franklin*, 27:623-27.

15. Labaree, *Papers of Benjamin Franklin*, 28:256-59.

16. Labaree, *Papers of Benjamin Franklin*, 37:184-96, 197, 206-7, 268, 373. Franklin even suspected the British of trying to poison him: Claude-Anne Lopez, *My Life with Benjamin Franklin* (New Haven: Yale University Press, 2000), 61-72.

17. Labaree, *Papers of Benjamin Franklin*, 37:72-76.

18. Dull, *French Navy and American Independence*, 238-48.

19. Labaree, *Papers of Benjamin Franklin*, 36:102n, 537n, 545-46, 684n; 37:25-30, 55-57, 69-70, 78, 113, 136-38, 140-44, 251-53, 316, 627. For Digges, see Robert H. Elias and Eugene D. Finch, eds., *Letters of Thomas Atwood Digges (1742-1821)* (Columbia: University of South Carolina Press, 1982).

20. Piers Mackesy, *The War for America, 1775-1783* (Cambridge: Harvard University Press, 1965), 434-36, 460-70.

21. Labaree, *Papers of Benjamin Franklin*, 35:161-67, 174-75; William C. Stinchcombe, *The American Revolution and the French Alliance* (Syracuse: Syracuse University Press, 1969), 153-69. The best discussion of the desperate condition of the United States in 1781 is Buel,

In Irons. See also Buel's marvelous *Dear Liberty: Connecticut's Mobilization for the Revolutionary War* (Middletown CT: Wesleyan University Press, 1980).

22. Labaree, *Papers of Benjamin Franklin*, 13:446–48; 14:242–43, 324–25, 331–32. In 1778 Shelburne had entertained an agent sent by the commissioners: Labaree, *Papers of Benjamin Franklin*, 25:234–35n; 26:158n.

23. Labaree, *Papers of Benjamin Franklin*, 37:17–18, 24–25, 102–4, 108, 155–59, 177–78, 234–36, 249–50, 281–82, 291–97. For the subsequent negotiations, see Labaree, *Papers of Benjamin Franklin*, 37:297–346 and following; 38: passim; Dull, *Franklin the Diplomat*, 53–60; Andrew Stockley, *Britain and France at the Birth of America: The European Powers and the Peace Negotiations of 1783–1783* (Exeter, Eng.: Exeter University Press, 2001); Vincent T. Harlow, *The Founding of the Second British Empire,* 1763–1793, 2 vols. (London: Longmans, Green, 1952–64), 1:223–311; Ronald Hoffman and Peter J. Albert, eds., *Peace and the Peacemakers: The Treaty of 1783* (Charlottesville: University Press of Virginia, 1986). Although informative, Richard Morris, *The Peacemakers: The Great Powers and American Independence* (New York: Harper and Row, 1965), is very biased against France and should be used with caution.

24. For Shelburne, see, in addition to the sources cited immediately above, C. Ritcheson, "The Earl of Shelburne and Peace with America, 1782–1783," *International History Review* 5 (1983): 322–45, and John Norris, *Shelburne and Reform* (London: Macmillan, 1963).

25. Labaree, *Papers of Benjamin Franklin*, 37:155–59, 163, 165–67, 169–72, 177–81, 184–85, 293–95.

26. Labaree, *Papers of Benjamin Franklin*, 37:136–37, 166–67, 177–80, 198, 201–2, 206, 243, 263, 288, 310, 343, 352, 377–80, 415–18, 477, 536–37, 623, 630–31.

27. Labaree, *Papers of Benjamin Franklin*, 37:235n, 270, 281–82, 298–305. Franklin kept a detailed journal of the negotiations prior to July 1: Labaree, *Papers of Benjamin Franklin*, 37:291–346. On May 29 he noted that Vergennes had told him that the Americans should negotiate for themselves, but for common security the treaties

should go hand in hand and be signed the same day: Labaree, *Papers of Benjamin Franklin*, 37:316.

28. Labaree, *Papers of Benjamin Franklin*, 37:306–9, 313–14, 318–28, 337–39, 421, 434–36.

29. Labaree, *Papers of Benjamin Franklin*, 37:598–602, 686–87; 38:85.

30. Labaree, *Papers of Benjamin Franklin*, 37:712–14; 38:30–32, 39–41, 82–83n, 92–93n, 113, 132n, 164. Franklin also suffered from periodical attacks of gout, which, in one of his wittiest bagatelles, he blamed on himself for failing to exercise: Labaree, *Papers of Benjamin Franklin*, 34:11–20.

31. Labaree, *Papers of Benjamin Franklin*, 38:191–92, 270–71; Dull, *French Navy and American Independence*, 302–16; Bradford Perkins, "The Peace of Paris: Patterns and Legacies," in Hoffman and Albert, *Peace and the Peacemakers*, 207–14.

32. Labaree, *Papers of Benjamin Franklin*, 38:164–67. During the negotiations Shelburne volunteered to arrange a meeting between William Temple Franklin and his father, but Temple refused: Labaree, *Papers of Benjamin Franklin*, 38:357n.

33. Labaree, *Papers of Benjamin Franklin*, 33:357; 38:92n, 257–60, 346–47, 350–56, 375–77, 382–88. After returning to America, Franklin advocated expansion in the Mississippi River area, preferably by purchase from Spain rather than conquest: Franklin to Charles Pettit, October 10, 1786 (Smyth, *Writings of Franklin*, 9:543–45).

34. Labaree, *Papers of Benjamin Franklin* , 38:459–62, 464–66, 606–8; Dull, *French Navy and American Independence*, 319–33. Terms for a separate British-Dutch treaty also were reached.

35. Labaree, *Papers of Benjamin Franklin*, 38:433–35, 444–45, 584–85.

36. Labaree, *Papers of Benjamin Franklin*, 38:584n; Giunta, *Emerging Nation*, 1:723, 765–66. George III also commented on Franklin's hatred of Britain: Sir John W. Fortescue, ed., *The Correspondence of King George the Third from 1760 to December, 1783*, 6 vols. (London: Macmillan, 1927–28), 4:80.

37. Labaree, *Papers of Benjamin Franklin*, 38:413; 39:63n, 120–22, 306–7; Buell, *In Irons*, 244–53.

38. Labaree, *Papers of Benjamin Franklin*, 38:151-53; 39:250-85, 300, 467.

39. Labaree, *Papers of Benjamin Franklin*, 38:128-29, 216-17, 577-78; 39:21, 108, 333-34, 348, 376-77, 391, 416-17, 448-49, 470-71, 477, 549-55, 564-68.

40. Labaree, *Papers of Benjamin Franklin*, 39:413n, 481-82, 524-26, 605-7. For postwar British-American relations, see Charles R. Ritcheson, *Aftermath of Revolution: British Policy toward the United States, 1783-1795* (Dallas: Southern Methodist University Press, 1969), and Frederick W. Marks III, *Independence on Trial: Foreign Affairs and the Making of the Constitution* (Baton Rouge: Louisiana State University Press, 1973).

41. Giunta, *Emerging Nation*, 2:803-11; Dumas Malone, *Jefferson and His Time*, 6 vols. (Boston: Little, Brown, 1948-81), 2:3-32.

42. Skemp, *William Franklin*, 270-71.

6. Franklin and His Fellow Americans

1. Labaree, *Papers of Benjamin Franklin*, 22:183n, 373n; 23:64n, 202n; 25:22, 417n; 27:229-33, 584; 30:548; 34:548n; 36:129n, 519-21; 37:172-73; Dull, *Franklin the Diplomat*, 33-40; Edmund S. Morgan, "The Puritan Ethic and the American Revolution," *William and Mary Quarterly*, 3rd series, 24 (1967): 3-43. Thomas Schaeper's forthcoming biography of Edward Bancroft corrects a number of misunderstandings about Deane.

2. Labaree, *Papers of Benjamin Franklin* , 24:243-45, 287-88, 294-96, 302-4, 322-25, 327-28, 338-39, 345-46, 394-95, 414-17, 468-70, 472-74, 482-83, 534-36, 549; 25:205, 478-79; Dull, *Franklin the Diplomat*, 23-25, 37-40; Clark, *Lambert Wickes*, 243-61; Robert Wilden Neeser, ed., *Letters and Papers Relating to the Cruises of Gustavus Conyngham, a Captain of the Continental Navy, 1777-1779* (New York: De Vinne Press for the Naval History Society, 1915).

3. The same was true of Arthur Lee's brother William, minister designate to Prussia and the Holy Roman Empire. See Labaree, *Papers of Benjamin Franklin* , 26:lxviii-lxix, 84, 129-30, 207-8, 215-16, 220-24, 231-35, 342-43, 355-58, 640-53; 27:448, 600; 28:517-21;

29:128–29, 599; 34:404, 519, 530–31; 35:473; Dull, *Franklin the Diplomat*, 15–17, 31. It was John Adams who compared American diplomats to militiamen: Dull, *Franklin the Diplomat*, 15.

4. Labaree, *Papers of Benjamin Franklin* , 29: lx–lxi, 186n, 370–71, 394–95, 490n; Butterfield, *Diary and Autobiography of John Adams*, 2:302, 304–5, 352, 363; 4:41, 86–88, 111–12.

5. Labaree, *Papers of Benjamin Franklin* , 28:461–64; 33:52–53, 141, 145, 162–63; 36:128; 38:165; 39:65n, 121, 128n, 301–2, 358, 562n, 569; Butterfield, *Diary and Autobiography of John Adams*, 2:367; L. H. Butterfield et al., eds., *Adams Family Correspondence*, 9 vols. to date (Cambridge: Belknap Press of Harvard University Press, 1963–), 5:250–52. The best critique of Adams's diplomacy, as well as one of the best books on the diplomacy of the American Revolution, is James H. Hutson, *John Adams and the Diplomacy of the American Revolution* (Lexington: University Press of Kentucky, 1980). For Vergennes' opinion of Adams, see Giunta, *Emerging Nation*, 1:936.

6. Labaree, *Papers of Benjamin Franklin*, 34:533; 37:713–14; 38:96–97, 220n, 275n, 388, 414, 451–52; Dull, *Franklin the Diplomat*, 58–59; Linda Grant De Pauw et al., eds., *Documentary History of the First Federal Congress of the United States of America, March 4, 1789, to March 3, 1791*, 17 vols. to date (Baltimore: Johns Hopkins University Press, 1972–), 2:252–71. For the Spanish contribution to American independence, see Thomas E. Chávez, *Spain and the Independence of the United States: An Intrinsic Gift* (Albuquerque: University of New Mexico Press, 2002).

7. Labaree, *Papers of Benjamin Franklin*, 38:347, 375; Philip M. Hamer et al., eds., *The Papers of Henry Laurens*, 16 vols. (Columbia: University of South Carolina Press, 1968–2003), 16:79–80.

8. Labaree, *Papers of Benjamin Franklin*, 34:244n, 280–81, 434n, 443–47; 35:28n, 103n, 174–75, 426–27; Dull, *Franklin the Diplomat*, 48–49; D. E. Huger Smith, ed., "The Mission of Col. John Laurens to Europe in 1781," *South Carolina Historical and Genealogical Magazine* 1 (1900): 13–41, 136–51, 213–22, 311–22; 2 (1901): 27–43, 108–25; James A. Lewis, *Neptune's Militia: The Frigate* South Carolina *during the American Revolution* (Kent OH: Kent State University Press, 1999).

There is an excellent recent biography of young Laurens, who was killed in a skirmish with a British foraging party near Charleston in 1782: Gregory D. Massey, *John Laurens and the American Revolution* (Columbia: University of South Carolina Press, 2000).

9. Labaree, *Papers of Benjamin Franklin,* 22:544n; 23:350-52; 24:3-4, 161-62n; 25:117; 26:lxvi-lxvii, 61-62, 107, 265-66, 307-8; 28:497-99; 32:155-58, 567n; 37:41-42; Dull, *Diplomatic History of the American Revolution*, 102, 126.

10. Labaree, *Papers of Benjamin Franklin*, 36:73.

11. Labaree, *Papers of Benjamin Franklin*, 29:180; 30:233-34; 31:291; 32:186, 354, 449-50.

12. Labaree, *Papers of Benjamin Franklin*, 27:600-601, 604; 29:599-600; 34:447-47; *Journals of the Continental Congress, 1774-1789*, 35 vols. (Washington DC: Government Printing Office, 1904-76), 5:827; 12:908; 20:647-48; 26:352; Henderson, *Party Politics*, 199-206.

13. In 1779 he survived a recall vote by eight states to two, but by 1781 his reputation had so declined that initially only four states voted to make him part of the peace commission, and it took a compromise to get him elected. Labaree, *Papers of Benjamin Franklin*, 35:162; Henderson, *Party Politics*, 296-303; Paul W. Smith et al., eds., *Letters of Delegates to Congress, 1774-1789*, 26 vols. (Washington DC: Library of Congress, 1976-2000), 17:320-21.

14. Franklin wrote Paine on September 27, 1785, soon after his return to America, to express his friendship: Smyth, *Writings of Franklin*, 9:467-68.

15. See Dull, *Age of the Ship of the Line*, 179-80 for a discussion of the point.

16. E. James Ferguson, *The Power of the Purse: A History of American Public Finance, 1776-1790* (Chapel Hill: University of North Carolina Press, 1961) and Buel, *In Irons* are indispensable economic histories of the war. Terry Bouton, *Taming Democracy: "The People," the Founders, and the Troubled Ending of the American Revolution* (Oxford: Oxford University Press, 2007) eloquently describes the terrible effects of Morris's deflationary policies on the common people of Pennsylvania, but because he does not discuss the hyperinflation that led to

Morris's rise to power, his account is very unbalanced. His portrait of Morris as concerned almost solely with his own self-interest is a caricature.

17. Labaree, *Papers of Benjamin Franklin*, 39:380–81.

18. Labaree, *Papers of Benjamin Franklin*, 39:380–85, 393–94.

EPILOGUE

1. For Franklin's anger at Britain's refusal to evacuate frontier posts (and his defense of America from British accusations), see his essay "The Retort Courteous," in Lemay, *Franklin: Writings*, 1122–30.

2. Robert L. Brunhouse, *The Counter-Revolution in Pennsylvania, 1776–1790* (Harrisburg: Pennsylvania Historical Commission, 1942), 125, 176–216.

3. Benjamin Rush to Richard Price, May 25, 1786, in L. H. Butterfield, ed., *Letters of Benjamin Rush*, 2 vols. (Princeton: Princeton University Press, 1951), 1:389–90.

4. A copy of the proclamation is at the Massachusetts Historical Society. For Franklin's disapproval of the rebellion, see also his April 19, 1787, letter to Thomas Jefferson in Julian P. Boyd et al., eds., *The Papers of Thomas Jefferson*, 36 vols. to date (Princeton: Princeton University Press, 1950–), 11:301–2.

5. William G. Carr, *The Oldest Delegate: Franklin in the Constitutional Convention* (Newark: University of Delaware Press; London: Associated University Presses, 1990), summarizes Franklin's activities at the convention. For his defense of the constitution against the Anti-Federalists, see Lemay, *Franklin: Writings*, 1144–48.

6. Waldstreicher, *Runaway America*, 229–39; Lemay, *Franklin: Writings*, 1154–60.

7. See the perceptive comments in Daniel Szechi, *1715: The Great Jacobite Rebellion* (New Haven: Yale University Press, 2006), 5.

Recommended Reading

In 1954 Yale University and the American Philosophical Society agreed to sponsor a complete edition of Benjamin Franklin's correspondence, and they appointed Leonard W. Labaree as its first chief editor. Labaree and his staff on the Franklin Papers began with the enormous task of finding and then photocopying or photographing all of the extant letters and documents sent to Franklin, sent by Franklin, or written by Franklin. Unlike the papers of the other founding fathers, Franklin's papers are widely scattered. Four repositories each hold more than 1,000 documents (the American Philosophical Society, the Library of Congress, the National Archives, and the Historical Society of Pennsylvania), while the remainder are located in thirty-two states, the District of Columbia, and thirteen foreign countries. The Papers of Benjamin Franklin has collected photographs or photocopies of some 30,000 letters and documents, including some duplicates, plus 2,200 printed documents of which usually the manuscript version is no longer extant. Photocopies of documents continue to arrive, thanks to the kindness of auction houses and the work of Franklin scholars. There are one or more extant pieces of Franklin's correspondence with more than 4,000 people. For more on this compilation, see Leonard W. Labaree et al., eds., *The Papers of Benjamin Franklin*, 39 vols. to date (New Haven: Yale University Press, 1959–), 1:xxxi–xxxiv; Leonard W. Labaree, "In Search of B. Franklin," *William and Mary Quarterly*, 3rd series, 16 (1959): 188–97; Leonard W. Labaree and Whitfield J. Bell, "The Papers of Benjamin Franklin: A Progress Report," *Proceedings of the American Philosophical Society* 101 (1957): 532–34; Franklin Papers accession file, Yale University.

The Papers of Benjamin Franklin is a nonprofit organization affiliated with the papers of other founding fathers (Washington, Jefferson, Madison, and the Adams family). It is supported by a combination of government and private grants. Its office is located in Sterling Memorial Library on the campus of Yale University. During my years with the project (1977–2008), its staff ranged between six and nine people. Visiting scholars are welcome, but most people rely on its chronologically arranged published edition, Labaree, *Papers of Benjamin Franklin*, which prints in full about 80 percent of the documents and describes or summarizes the remainder; documents in English or French are printed in the original language, while those in Italian, German, Latin, or other languages are translated into English. Leonard W. Labaree et al., eds., *The Autobiography of Benjamin Franklin* (New Haven: Yale University Press, 1964, rev. ed., 2003) is published separately. The series at present is complete through May 15, 1783; the next four volumes will cover Franklin's remaining years in France and will be followed by four volumes covering the final years of his life. The best edition for the years not yet covered is Albert H. Smyth, ed., *The Writings of Benjamin Franklin*, 10 vols. (New York: Macmillan; London: Macmillan, 1905–7). On the internet are uncorrected transcripts of the remaining documents, as well as transcripts of roughly 20 percent of the documents from the French period not published in full; go to *www.franklinpapers.org.*

There also are three single-volume editions giving a selection of Franklin's correspondence. The largest is J. A. Leo Lemay, ed., *Benjamin Franklin* (New York: Library of America, 1987). The others are Edmund S. Morgan, ed., *Not Your Usual Founding Father: Selected Readings from Benjamin Franklin* (New Haven: Yale University Press, 2006) and Walter Isaacson, ed., *A Benjamin Franklin Reader* (New York: Simon and Schuster, 2003).

Knowledge of the Continental Congress is vital to understanding both the American Revolution and Franklin's place in it. The records of the Continental Congress are available on 220 reels of microfilm. Fortunately, there is an index to them: John P. Butler, comp., *The Papers of the Continental Congress, 1774–1789: Index*, 5 vols. (Washington DC: Government Printing Office, 1978). The official proceedings of Congress have been published as *Journals of the Continental Congress, 1774–1789*, 35 vols. (Washington DC: Government Printing Office, 1904–76). The most recent edition of selected documents relating to American diplomacy is Mary A. Giunta et al., eds., *The Emerging Nation: A Documentary History of the Foreign Relations of the United States under the Articles of Confederation, 1780–1789*, 3 vols. (Washington

DC: National Historical Publications and Records Commission, 1996). It, however, does not include all the documents in Francis Wharton, ed., *The Revolutionary Diplomatic Correspondence of the United States*, 6 vols. (Washington DC: Government Printing Office, 1889). The most useful collection of documents relating to diplomacy during the early part of the war is B. F. Stevens, comp., *Facsimiles of Manuscripts in European Archives Relating to America, 1773–1783*, 25 vols. (London: privately printed, 1889–98). Henri Doniol, *Histoire de la participation de la France à l'établissement des Etats-Unis d'Amérique: Correspondance diplomatique et documents*, 5 vols. plus supplementary volume (Paris: Imprimerie Nationale, 1886–99), must be used with caution because the documents it selects sometimes are taken out of context. John J. Meng, ed., *Despatches and Instructions of Conrad Alexandre Gérard, 1778–1780* (Baltimore: Johns Hopkins University Press, 1939), however, is excellent.

Two editions treat naval affairs during the period: William B. Clark et al., eds., *Naval Documents of the American Revolution*, 11 vols. to date (Washington DC: Government Printing Office, 1964–) and Robert Wilden Neeser, ed., *Letters and Papers Relating to the Cruises of Gustavus Conyngham, Captain of the Continental Navy, 1777–1779* (New York: De Vinne Press for the Naval History Society, 1915).

There are many documentary collections relating to Franklin's contemporaries. Often these shed light on Franklin's life. The most wide-ranging is Paul H. Smith et al., eds., *Letters of Delegates to Congress, 1774–1789*, 26 vols. (Washington DC: Library of Congress, 1976–2000).

Another extremely well edited and important edition is that of the powerful American finance minister: E. James Ferguson et al., eds., *The Papers of Robert Morris, 1781–1784*, 9 vols. (Pittsburgh: University of Pittsburgh Press, 1973–99).

Franklin's first two colleagues in France were Arthur Lee and Silas Deane. Lee's papers are available on microfilm as part of Paul P. Hoffman, ed., *The Lee Family Papers, 1742–1795*, 8 reels (Charlottesville: University of Virginia microfilm publication no. 1, 1966). There are two editions of Deane's papers. The larger, *The Deane Papers, 1774–1790*, appeared as volumes 19–24 of the *Collections of the New-York Historical Society* (New York, 1886–90). The smaller, *The Deane Papers: Correspondence between Silas Deane, His Brothers, and Their Business and Political Associates, 1771–1795*, appeared as volume 23 of the *Connecticut Historical Society Collections* (Hartford, 1930).

Franklin was joined in France in 1778 by John Adams. The correspondence of the Adams family, which is available on microfilm from the Massachusetts Historical Society, is being published in several series, three of which are relevant to his diplomatic missions: L. H. Butterfield et al., eds., *Diary and Autobiography of John Adams*, 4 vols. (Cambridge: Belknap Press of the Harvard University Press, 1961); L. H. Butterfield et al., eds., *Adams Family Correspondence*, 9 vols. to date (Cambridge: Belknap Press of the Harvard University Press, 1963–); and Robert J. Taylor et al., eds., *Papers of John Adams*, 15 vols. to date (Cambridge: Belknap Press of the Harvard University Press, 1977–).

The peace negotiations of 1782 were conducted by Franklin, Adams, and John Jay. Jay's papers were published as Henry P. Johnston, ed., *The Correspondence and Public Papers of John Jay*, 4 vols. (New York: G. P. Putnam's Sons, 1890–93). This collection has been largely but not completely replaced by two volumes of selected documents: Richard B. Morris et al., eds., *John Jay: The Making of a Revolutionary; Unpublished Papers, 1745–1780* (New York: Harper and Row, 1975) and *John Jay: The Winning of the Peace; Unpublished Papers, 1780–1784* (New York: Harper and Row, 1980). At the last moment the American peace commissioners were joined by Henry Laurens. A highly selective edition of his papers has been published as Philip M. Hamer et al., eds., *The Papers of Henry Laurens*, 16 vols. (Columbia: University of South Carolina Press, 1968–2003). Franklin's final diplomatic colleague was Thomas Jefferson, whose papers are published in three series, one devoted to his public life, one devoted to special topics, and one devoted to his retirement years. The first of these is Julian P. Boyd et al., eds., *The Papers of Thomas Jefferson*, 36 vols. to date (Princeton: Princeton University Press, 1950–).

Franklin also appears in passing in numerous other documentary editions, including Eric Foner, ed., *The Complete Writings of Thomas Paine*, 2 vols. (New York: Citadel Press, 1945); Sir John W. Fortescue, ed., *The Correspondence of King George the Third from 1760 to December 1783*, 6 vols. (London: Macmillan, 1927–28); W. W. Abbot et al., eds., *The Papers of George Washington: Revolutionary War Series*, 19 vols. to date (Charlottesville: University Press of Virginia, 1985–); William T. Hutchinson et al., eds., *The Papers of James Madison*, 1st series, 17 vols. (Chicago: University of Chicago Press; Charlottesville: University Press of Virginia, 1962–91); W. Bernard Peach and D. O. Thomas, eds., *The Correspondence of Richard Price*, 3 vols. (Durham NC: Duke University Press; Cardiff: University of Wales Press, 1982–94); Robert H. Elias and Eugene D. Finch, eds., *Letters of Thomas Atwood Digges (1742–1821)* (Columbia: University of South Carolina Press, 1982); Stanley J. Idzerda et al., eds., *Lafayette in the Age of the American Revolution: Selected Letters and Papers, 1776–1790*, 5 vols. to date (Ithaca NY: Cornell University Press, 1977–); Ronald Hofmann et al., eds., *Dear Papa, Dear Charley: The Peregrinations of a Revolutionary Aristocrat, as Told by Charles Carroll of Carrollton and His Father, Charles Carroll of Annapolis*, 3 vols. (Chapel Hill: University of North Carolina Press, 2001); Worthington Chauncey Ford, ed., *Letters of William Lee, Sheriff and Alderman of London: Commercial Agent of the Continental Congress in France; and Minister to the Courts of Vienna and Berlin, 1776–1783*, 3 vols. (Brooklyn: Historical Printing Club, 1891). A disappointingly meager source is John Hardman and Munro Price, eds., *Louis XVI and the Comte de Vergennes, Correspondence, 1774–1783* (Oxford: Voltaire Foundation, 1998), although the editors' introduction contains a lengthy discussion of the American alliance. Both editors have written major works on Louis XVI and on French court politics during his reign.

There are many biographies of Franklin and his contemporaries. I will mention some of those most relevant to the topic of the present book. For a detailed annotated bibliography of books and articles relating to Franklin and published between 1721 and 1983, consult Melvin H. Buxbaum, comp., *Benjamin Franklin: A Reference Guide*, 2 vols. (Boston: G. K. Hall, 1983–88). Michael Zuckerman reviews recent work in "Benjamin Franklin at 300: The Show Goes On: A Review of the Reviews," *Pennsylvania Magazine of History and Biography* 131 (2007): 177–207.

My favorite biography of Franklin is by the late J. A. Leo Lemay: *The Life of Benjamin Franklin*, 3 vols. (Philadelphia: University of Pennsylvania Press, 2006–9). It was intended to contain 7 volumes, finally providing a comprehensive multivolume biography comparable to such classics as Dumas Malone, *Jefferson and His Time*, 6 vols. (Boston: Little, Brown, 1948–81), but with Lemay's death it ends in 1757. For the latter period of Franklin's life we are still dependent on single-volume biographies, studies of Franklin's thought and character, and specialized studies of his accomplishments in science, literature, politics, diplomacy, and other fields.

Several short biographies have been published over the last twenty-five years. Esmond Wright, *Franklin of Philadelphia* (Cambridge: Belknap Press of Harvard University Press, 1986) is a perceptive account of Franklin's life, although not as well informed about his times as are several more recent biographies. Walter Isaacson, *Benjamin Franklin: An American Life* (New York: Simon and Schuster, 2003) is particularly good on Franklin's impact on American culture. H. W. Brands, *The First American: The Life and Times of Benjamin Franklin* (New York: Doubleday, 2000) is a well-rounded introduction by a veteran biographer. Edmund S. Morgan, *Benjamin Franklin* (New Haven: Yale University Press, 2002) is a charming brief biography.

Several recent biographical essays treat Franklin's life from a particular perspective. Three are especially bracing and well written: Robert Middlekauff, *Benjamin Franklin and His Enemies* (Berkeley: University of California Press, 1996), Gordon S. Wood, *The Americanization of Benjamin Franklin* (New York: Penguin Press, 2004), and David Waldstreicher, *Runaway America: Benjamin Franklin, Slavery, and the American Revolution* (New York: Hill and Wang, 2004).

Franklin's private life is ably covered by Claude-Anne Lopez and Eugenia Herbert, *The Private Franklin: The Man and His Family* (New York: Norton, 1975) and Sheila Skemp, *William Franklin: Son of a Patriot, Servant of a King* (New York: Oxford University Press, 1990).

Other works specialize in a particular period of Franklin's life. For his years as a Pennsylvania politician and colonial agent, see William S. Hanna, *Benjamin Franklin and Pennsylvania Politics* (Stanford: Stanford University Press, 1964), James H. Hutson, *Pennsylvania Politics, 1746–1760: The Movement for Royal Government and Its Consequences* (Princeton: Princeton University Press, 1972), and Benjamin H. Newcomb, *Franklin and Galloway: A Political Partnership* (New Haven: Yale University Press, 1962). Jack P. Greene, *Understanding the American Revolution: Issues and Actions* (Charlottesville: University Press of Virginia, 1995) contains two articles by Greene on Franklin's radicalization by his English experiences: "Pride, Prejudice, and Jealousy: Benjamin Franklin's

Explanation of the American Revolution" and "The Alienation of Benjamin Franklin, British American"; see also William B. Willcox, "Franklin's Last Years in England: The Making of a Rebel," in Melvin H. Buxbaum, ed., *Critical Essays on Benjamin Franklin* (Boston: G. K. Hall, 1987), 96–110. For his activities as a colonial agent, see David T. Morgan, *The Devious Dr. Franklin, Colonial Agent: Benjamin Franklin's Years in London* (Macon GA: Mercer University Press, 1996) and Michael J. Kammen, *A Rope of Sand: The Colonial Agents, British Politics, and the American Revolution* (Ithaca: Cornell University Press, 1968). His service in Congress is mentioned in many books but has not yet received the attention it merits; see, however, vol. 22 of Labaree, *Papers of Benjamin Franklin*. His mission to France is the subject of a number of books, including my *Franklin the Diplomat: The French Mission* (Philadelphia: American Philosophical Society, 1982 [as *Transactions of the American Philosophical Society*, vol. 72, part 1]), which treats his diplomatic activities in more detail than does the present book; Stacy Schiff, *A Great Improvisation: Franklin, France, and the Birth of America* (New York: Henry Holt, 2005); and Claude-Anne Lopez, *Mon Cher Papa: Franklin and the Ladies of Paris* (New Haven: Yale University Press, 1962). Alfred Owen Aldridge, *Franklin and His French Contemporaries* (New York: New York University Press, 1957) is interesting but rather dated. William Bell Clark, *Ben Franklin's Privateers: A Naval Epic of the American Revolution* (Baton Rouge: Louisiana State University Press, 1956) details how Franklin attempted to procure British prisoners of war to exchange for American prisoners in England.

Franklin's final years are perhaps the most neglected period of his life; indeed, the staff of the Papers of Benjamin Franklin is still collecting documents. There is, however, a book on his service in the Constitutional Convention: William G. Carr, *The Oldest Delegate: Franklin in the Constitutional Convention* (Newark: University of Delaware Press; London: Associated University Presses, 1990).

Four fine books about Franklin deal with the foundations of his political and diplomatic philosophy: Paul W. Conner, *Poor Richard's Politicks: Benjamin Franklin and the New American Order* (New York: Oxford University Press, 1966), Lorraine Smith Pangle, *The Political Philosophy of Benjamin Franklin* (Baltimore: Johns Hopkins University Press, 2007), Alan Houston, *Benjamin Franklin and the Politics of Improvement* (New Haven: Yale University Press, 2008), and Gerald Stourzh, *Benjamin Franklin and American Foreign Policy*, 2nd ed. (Chicago: University of Chicago Press, 1969). A good introduction to his social and economic ideas is Drew McCoy, "Benjamin Franklin's Vision of a Republican Political Economy for America," *William and Mary Quarterly*, 3rd series, 35 (1978): 605–28. To understand the intellectual climate in which he flourished, read Henry F. May, *The Enlightenment in America* (New York: Oxford University Press, 1976).

Since Franklin interacted with virtually every important person in the American Revolution, it would require many pages to discuss their biographies. Thus I will restrict myself to calling attention to a few of them. Arthur Lee is the subject of a fine book: Louis W. Potts,

Arthur Lee, a Virtuous Revolutionary (Baton Rouge: Louisiana State University Press, 1981); see also a biography of one of Lee's secretaries: John R. Alden, *Stephen Sayre: American Revolutionary Adventurer* (Baton Rouge: Louisiana State University Press, 1983). There is much information about Franklin in a superb study of Congress's commercial representative, Thomas Barclay: Priscilla H. and Richard S. Roberts, *Thomas Barclay (1728–1793): Consul in France, Diplomat in Barbary* (Bethlehem PA: Lehigh University Press, 2008). Walter Stahr, *John Jay, Founding Father* (New York: Hambledon and London, 2005) is a long-needed modern biography. Kalman Goldstein, "Silas Deane: Preparation for Rascality," *Historian* 43 (1980–81): 75–97 is the best introduction to Deane. For Franklin's nemesis, see Jeremy Black, *George III: America's Last King* (New Haven: Yale University Press, 2006). Brian N. Morton and Donald Spinelli, *Beaumarchais and the American Revolution* (Latham MD: Lexington Books, 2003) corrects misapprehensions about the playwright and arms dealer with whom the commissioners dealt. Two of the most important Frenchmen to Franklin were his landlord Chaumont and Foreign Minister Vergennes, who have each received an English-language biography: Thomas J. Schaeper, *France and America in the Revolutionary Era: The Life of Jacques Donatien Leray de Chaumont* (Providence RI: Berghahn Books, 1995) and Orville T. Murphy, *Charles Gravier de Vergennes: French Diplomacy in the Age of Revolution, 1719–1787* (Albany: State University of New York Press, 1975). There are many biographies of John Adams. I am particularly impressed by two relatively short books: James H. Hutson, *John Adams and the Diplomacy of the American Revolution* (Lexington: University Press of Kentucky, 1980) and Peter Shaw, *The Character of John Adams* (Chapel Hill: University of North Carolina Press, 1976).

In spite of the enormous number of biographies, there is still work to be done. The most obvious gaps relating to Franklin are the lack of biographies of Jonathan Williams Jr., Franklin's most frequent correspondent while he was in France, and of William Temple Franklin. A modern biography of William Carmichael would be very useful, and more needs to be done on Silas Deane and Henry Laurens. Thomas Schaeper's forthcoming biography of Edward Bancroft promises to fill another major gap.

Finally I would like to suggest a few of the many thousands of books on the American Revolution. The major debate in the field is between those who see it as a social revolution marked by widespread class conflict and those who see it as predominantly a cultural and ideological conflict. A good introduction to the dispute is to read surveys of the period by leading members of each camp. I suggest comparing Gary B. Nash, *The Unknown American Revolution: The Unruly Birth of Democracy and the Struggle to Create America* (New York: Viking, 2005) and Gordon S. Wood, *The Radicalism of the American Revolution* (New York: Alfred A. Knopf, 1992). Not all surveys fall neatly within the two categories, however. One interesting approach is T. G. Barrow, "The American Revolution as a Colonial War for Independence," *William and Mary Quarterly*, 3rd series, 25 (1968): 452–64.

It is difficult to impose a structure on American political history during the Revolution because political groupings were very fluid and disorderly. Marc Egnal, *A Mighty Empire: The Origins of the American Revolution* (Ithaca: Cornell University Press, 1988) finds the beginnings of political factions, if not parties, before the Revolution began. H. James Henderson, *Party Politics in the Continental Congress* (New York: McGraw-Hill, 1974) assigns delegates to the Continental Congress to different shifting factions. In contrast to this schematic approach, Jack N. Rakove, *The Beginnings of National Politics: An Interpretive History of the Continental Congress* (New York: Alfred A. Knopf, 1979) adopts a narrative approach. Edmund S. Morgan, "The Puritan Ethic and the American Revolution," *William and Mary Quarterly*, 3rd series, 24 (1967): 3–43, uses the debate over Silas Deane's conduct in France (among other incidents) as a case study of congressional divisions. Edmund Cody Burnett, *The Continental Congress* (New York: Macmillan, 1941) is still useful as a straightforward account of what transpired in Congress. Irving Brant, *James Madison: The Nationalist, 1780–7* (Indianapolis: Bobbs-Merrill, 1948), part of a multivolume biography, is extremely informative about Congress.

Diplomacy was a major subject of debate in Congress. Three important works on this subject are Felix Gilbert, *To the Farewell Address: Ideas of Early American Foreign Policy* (Princeton: Princeton University Press, 1969), James H. Hutson, "Intellectual Foundations of Early America Diplomacy," *Diplomatic History* 1 (1977): 1–19, and William C. Stinchcombe, *The American Revolution and the French Alliance* (Syracuse: Syracuse University Press, 1969). Other authors have dealt with the Revolution as an aspect of the diplomatic history of the era, particularly Samuel Flagg Bemis, *The Diplomacy of the American Revolution*, rev. ed. (Bloomington: Indiana University Press, 1957) and my own book, *A Diplomatic History of the American Revolution* (New Haven: Yale University Press, 1985).

One of the chief concerns of Congress was finance. E. James Ferguson, *The Power of the Purse: A History of American Public Finance, 1776–1790* (Chapel Hill: University of North Carolina Press, 1961) provides the best introduction.

Much of American political life took place on the state level. A good survey is Jackson Turner Main, *The Sovereign States, 1775–1783* (New York: New Viewpoints, 1973). Most relevant to Franklin, of course, is Pennsylvania, for which see Richard A. Ryerson, *"The Revolution Is Now Begun": The Radical Committees of Philadelphia, 1765–1776* (Philadelphia: University of Pennsylvania Press, 1978), Douglas M. Arnold, *A Republican Revolution: Ideology and Politics in Pennsylvania, 1776–1790* (New York: Garland, 1989), Robert A. Brunhouse, *The Counter-Revolution in Pennsylvania, 1776–1790* (Harrisburg: Pennsylvania Historical Commission, 1992), and Terry Bouton, *Taming Democracy: "The People," the Founders, and the Troubled Ending of the American Revolution* (Oxford: Oxford University Press, 2007).

Books on the British and French perspectives on the Revolution are included in the bibliographies of my book *The French Navy and American Independence: A Study of Arms and Diplomacy, 1774–1787* (Princeton: Princeton University Press, 1975), 379–423, and of my *Diplomatic*

History of the American Revolution, 175–218, although a number of books have appeared since the latter was published in 1985. Two of the most important are H. M. Scott, *British Foreign Policy in the Age of the American Revolution* (Oxford: Clarendon Press; New York: Oxford University Press, 1990), and Brendan Simms, *Three Victories and a Defeat: The Rise and Fall of the First British Empire* (London: Allen Lane, 2007; New York: Basic Books, 2008). My favorite military history of the war still is Piers Mackesy, *The War for America, 1775–1783* (Cambridge: Harvard University Press, 1965).

In 1978 the Capitol Historical Society sponsored a conference on the Franco-American alliance. Its proceedings were published as Ronald Hoffman and Peter J. Albert, eds., *Diplomacy and Revolution: The Franco-American Alliance of 1778* (Charlottesville: University Press of Virginia, 1981). Hoffman and Albert also edited the proceedings of a similar conference held a few years later, *Peace and the Peacemakers: The Treaty of 1783* (Charlottesville: University Press of Virginia, 1986). Other works dealing with the 1782–83 peace negotiations include Vincent T. Harlow, *The Founding of the Second British Empire, 1763–1793*, vol. 1 (London: Longmans, Green, 1952), Andrew Stockley, *Britain and France at the Birth of America: The European Powers and the Peace Negotiations of 1782–1783* (Exeter, Eng.: Exeter University Press, 2001), and the informative but biased Richard Morris, *The Peacemakers: The Great Powers and American Independence* (New York: Harper and Row, 1965).

Additional books on various topics relating to Franklin are listed in the endnotes.

Index

Previous Books by Jonathan R. Dull

The French Navy and American Independence:
A Study of Arms and Diplomacy, 1774–1787
(Princeton NJ: Princeton University Press, 1975)

Franklin the Diplomat: The French Mission
(Philadelphia: American Philosophical Society, 1982)

A Diplomatic History of the American Revolution
(New Haven: Yale University Press, 1985)

The French Navy and the Seven Years' War
(Lincoln: University of Nebraska Press, 2005)

The Age of the Ship of the Line:
The British and French Navies, 1650–1815
(Lincoln: University of Nebraska Press, 2009)